HOW TO CHOP TOPS

A Pictorial Guide to Hot Rodding's Most Popular Modification

Tony Thacker

CarTech®

CarTech®

CarTech®, Inc.
6118 Main Street
North Branch, MN 55056
Phone: 651-277-1200 or 800-551-4754
Fax: 651-277-1203
www.cartechbooks.com

Edit by Bob Wilson
Layout by Connie DeFlorin

ISBN 978-1-61325-605-3
Item No. SA508

Library of Congress Cataloging-in-Publication Data Available

Written, edited, and designed in the U.S.A.
Printed in China
10 9 8 7 6 5 4 3 2 1

CarTech books may be purchased at a discounted rate in bulk for resale, events, corporate gifts, or educational purposes. Special editions may also be created to specification. For details, contact Special Sales at 6118 Main Street, North Branch, MN 55056 or by email at sales@cartechbooks.com.

DISTRIBUTION BY:

Europe
PGUK
63 Hatton Garden
London EC1N 8LE, England
Phone: 020 7061 1980 • Fax: 020 7242 3725
www.pguk.co.uk

Australia
Renniks Publications Ltd.
3/37-39 Green Street
Banksmeadow, NSW 2109, Australia
Phone: 2 9695 7055 • Fax: 2 9695 7355
www.renniks.com

Canada
Login Canada
300 Saulteaux Crescent
Winnipeg, MB, R3J 3T2 Canada
Phone: 800 665 1148 • Fax: 800 665 0103
www.lb.ca

CONTENTS

Acknowledgments..4
Introduction...5
Chapter 1: Tools and Equipment 16
Chapter 2: Ford Model Ts 22
Chapter 3: Rick and Rayce Lefever: Ford Model A 26
Chapter 4: Veazie Bros. Fabrication: Bruce Fortie's 1932 Ford 3-Window Coupe 39
Chapter 5: The Kennedy Brothers: Two 1932 Ford 3-Window Coupes and a 1932 Ford 5-Window Coupe ... 63
Chapter 6: Walden Speed Shop: 1932 Ford 5-Window Coupe 81
Chapter 7: Hollywood Hot Rods: 1933 Ford 3-Window Coupe 89
Chapter 8: Rolling Bones: Schmidt & Suckling 1934 Coupe 117
Chapter 9: Roy Brizio Street Rods: Jeff Beck's 1934 Ford 5-Window Coupe 130
Chapter 10: 1936 Ford 3-Window Coupes 137
Chapter 11: Cornfield Customs: 1940 Cadillac LaSalle Model 50 145
Chapter 12: Pete and Jake's Hot Rod Parts: Billy F Gibbons's 1950 Ford Shoebox *Kopperhed* 150
Chapter 13: Fabian Valdez: 1950 Chevy Styleline 156
Chapter 14: Max Grundy: 1960 Dodge Dart Phoenix and 1961 Chrysler Newport 160
Chapter 15: Glass Cutting 173
Source Guide **176**

ACKNOWLEDGMENTS

Writing a how-to book is not an easy task. Documenting top chops required patience and cooperation from the builders. At the top of my thank-you list is Katie Sloan-Steele, who always goes above and beyond with her research—I really appreciate your help. Secondly, thanks to all of the builders and their staff who have been patient with my demands to "just do that again, please." Thanks to Mick Jenkins at Mick's Paint, who puts up with my endless questions and need for help. Finally, thanks to my wife and daughter, as they put up with it all. If I've missed anyone, I apologize.

Thanks to Brett Barris, Chris Blattie (Montana Glass), Roy Brizio, Larry Erickson, Billy F Gibbons, Max Grundy, Troy Ladd and his team at Hollywood Hot Rods (Kyle Connole, Marco Luz, Brian Sloma, and Geoff Wheeless), Randy Lorentzen, Thom Taylor, Steve Stanford, Bruce Fortie, Jay and Joe Kennedy, Rick and Rayce Lefever, Bob Marianich, Beth and Ross Meyers (3 Dog Garage), Ken Schmidt (Rolling Bones), David Steele and Jim Miller (American Hot Rod Foundation), Jon Suckling, Fabian Valdez, Evin and Justin Veazie, Bobby Walden (Walden Speed Shop), Debbri Wraga, Joel Davis (Davis Haus of Style), and Mike Wagner (Cornfield Customs).

Many years ago, I was at a car event when someone asked me why hot rodders chopped tops instead of raising them, which, as he said, would improve visibility. I guess that it would improve visibility, but that's completely missing the point. Chopping a top is not about visibility in that sense. Instead, it's about making a visual statement.

There's always one exception to the rule, and in this case, the exception was Steve Scott's *Uncertain-T*. The car, which began as a cartoon when Scott was just 17 in 1960, debuted in 1965 and was featured in the November 1965 issue of *Car Craft* magazine. Winning a special Sweepstakes Award at the Winternationals Car Show caused a furor in the show scene when

George Barris allegedly attacked Scott because of his win. The *Uncertain-T* still exists, but the car that is shown in this book is a tribute that was built in New Zealand by Martin Bennett.

Before World War II, coupes and sedans were barely regarded as hot rods. Roadsters were hot rods, and coupes were for chickens. Indeed, the Southern California Timing Association (SCTA), which was formed late in 1937, specifically banned coupes and sedans. However, the Russetta Timing Association (RTA) as well as the Western Timing Association (WTA) allowed coupes to race (as did the SCTA eventually).

"We didn't think coupes were real hot rods," said Alex Xydias, who was on the SCTA board at the time. "At

first, we didn't even believe the numbers. Of course, when Baney and the Pierson's [coupes] started going fast, we had to give in. I actually recruited Bob Pierson to run under the Side-winders banner so that we could win the points championship one year."

Another reason that closed cars were not as popular as roadsters was that they were generally more expensive. According to Don Montgomery in his book *Hot Rods as They Were: Another Blast from the Past*, the 1935 value of a standard 1932 roadster was $225, whereas a 1932 Ford Deluxe four-door sedan was $275. Besides, roadsters were cool and lighter. For example, a 1932 V-8 roadster weighed 2,242 pounds, whereas a 1932 3-window De Luxe coupe weighed 2,464 pounds (more than 200 pounds of additional weight). With most racers running flathead Ford V-8s, they all had similar power, so the weight made a big difference.

According to the January 1941 issue of *Throttle*, at the last Muroc WTA event of 1940, Eldon Shimmin, driving a 1939 Mercury convertible, set the coupe class record at 107.48 mph. It wasn't chopped—it looked stock, but under the hood it sported a hot motor. There was only one other coupe mentioned in the first 12 issues of *Throttle*. When *Hot Rod* was launched in January 1948, it was no different, as the only coupe mentioned in the first issue was Don Brown's 1936 coupe that ran 115.97 mph at a Russetta meet.

Things changed after World War II, when returning service men and women were looking for the

One of the few hot rods that has bigger-than-stock windows is Steve Scott's cartoon-inspired Uncertain-T *of 1965. This is the latter-day tribute car that was built in New Zealand by Martin Bennett and displayed at the 2020 Grand National Roadster Show.*

Master engine builder Don Towle was a member of the Russetta Coupes Club and worked for Edelbrock. His 1934 5-window coupe features "Edelbrock Equip" on the hood, blanked-out rear side windows, and an aerodynamic nose. Don Corwin drove the car in 1948 and 1949, setting a record at 135.85 mph.

excitement that hot rodding provided and there just didn't seem to be enough roadsters to go around. Hence, the general acceptance of coupes (and sedans to a lesser extent) followed. In that January 1948 inaugural issue of *Hot Rod*, I found small advertisements from the Barris Brothers Custom Shop, Carson Top Shop, and Jimmy Summers. In the February 1948 issue, Al Wallace's Custom Body Shop at 4822 Santa Monica Blvd. advertised complete custom work, including chopped tops, push-button doors, and custom lacquer painting.

The trend was catching on, and in late 1948, Bob Pierson appeared in the Russetta results. This would be prophetic. Bob ran 117.03 mph in his A-class, Edelbrock-equipped, 1946 Mercury–powered 1936 Ford 3-window coupe.

There were others—but not many. Meanwhile, Pierson's coupe became the cover car and the Hot Rod of the Month in the August 1948 issue of *Hot Rod*. While the 1936 coupe was unchopped, the article predicted that, "In the future, a new car will be built, embodying the best points of this car with certain improvements. The car will be chopped . . ."

Indeed, in 1949, the 1936 coupe was chopped, and it ran 140 mph in 1950, after which it was retired.

No other coupes and no sedans appeared in the first year of *Hot Rod's* publication with the exception of Fran Hernandez's stock-height 1932 3-window coupe and Don Towle's chopped 1934 coupe that clocked over 115 mph at a Russetta meet on Aug. 15, 1948. The car was actually driven by Don Corwin, and when the belly pan was modified, the speed was increased to 135.85 mph, running an Edelbrock-equipped Mercury.

In total, 28 coupes ran at that meet, and by the end of the season, November-meet speeds had increased dramatically. Pierson ran 120.32 mph in A class, Lou Baney ran 123.11 mph in B class, and Hernandez ran 119.20 mph in C class. Don Brown held the record at 123.12 mph. Baney's 5-window coupe was chopped and the die was set.

Meanwhile, on the street, there was Earle Bruce and his chopped 1940 Ford Deluxe Business coupe. The flathead engine of Bruce's coupe was featured on the cover of *Hot Rod* in February 1952 as "California's Most Customized Coupe." Bruce purchased the car brand new in late 1939 and immediately had it chopped 3½ inches. Bruce bought the car from Al Stuebing Ford on Cahuenga Boulevard in Los Angeles.

Bruce, who at one time owned the Big Top bar at 5336 Sunset Blvd. in Hollywood, had just signed a seven-year contract with 20th Century Fox and was paid $1,000. Almost immediately, Bruce drove the car to Jimmy Summers's shop on the corner of Melrose Avenue and Fairfax (7919 Melrose Ave.). According to an interview in *American Rodder* magazine, Bruce told Summers: "Cut the son-of-a-bitch, I ordered 4¾ inches. Reshape the top, fill in the rear side window, make the back window smaller . . .

"Since World War II was warming up, perhaps you can do all of this before I receive a letter from Franklin D. Roosevelt that begins with 'Greetings.'"

Bruce said that he christened his creation the *Armored Car* because it was all hammered metal with no lead filler.

Bruce's 1940 coupe may not have been the first chopped car on the scene, but it was certainly one of the first, and Bruce owned the car until his passing in 2009 at age 91. Meanwhile, in Lynwood, California, the Barris Brothers (George and Sam) were making history cutting the tops of everything that parked on Atlantic Boulevard. George was also accused of slapping a Barris crest on anything that parked there for more than two hours, but that's another story. The brothers started out at 7674 Compton Ave. in Los Angeles but moved to 11054 S. Atlantic Blvd. in Lynwood in 1950.

Although regarded as the marketer, George was no slouch when it came to metalwork or paintwork. However, it was his older brother Sam who excelled when he chopped his own 1949 Mercury. This wasn't the first chop that Sam had executed, but it was regarded as his seminal piece that set the style for everything that followed.

By the time Sam got to his own Mercury, he'd cut several 1930s and 1940s cars, so he had practiced his technique. In addition, he may have already cut Jerry Quesnel's 1949 Mercury, as there is photographic evidence from an album created by Marcia Campbell that Sam cut Quesnel's top just weeks before his own, affording him valuable experience.

There are two major differences between the Quesnel Mercury and the Barris Mercury. The Barris Mercury has a vertical B-pillar, whereas the Quesnel Mercury has the B-pillar raked forward. In addition, Barris gave his car a full fadeaway, removing the dog leg in the side pressing, and Quesnel's car did not have that area filled. Both cars, of course, had split windshields with flat glass.

Regardless of whose car was first, Sam began by cutting the roof off the car. Then he sectioned the pillars, moved the roof forward until the A-pillar aligned, and then laid the rear window down before he filled the gaps, often using the parts that had been removed. However, that is grossly oversimplifying the process.

Cars of the late 1930s and 1940s often had roof inserts and flat glass, which made the chopping task easier

In January 1948, the publication of Hot Rod *magazine gave auto-body men, such as Jimmy Summers, the ability to advertise to a large audience. Located on Melrose Avenue, Summers was in Hollywood.*

than it became on later models with curved roofs and curved glass. However, by that time, the chopping process had improved.

While Sam's Mercury didn't make it to the cover of *Hot Rod*, (it was featured on the cover of the December 1951 issue of *MotorTrend* magazine), the first chopped car to appear on the cover of *Hot Rod* was Jack Calori's beautiful chopped 1936 coupe for the November 1949 issue. In 1947, Calori bought the car from its original owner and used it to tow his lakes-racing roadster. He stored it in his friend Herb Reneau's garage. Without much discussion, Reneau hacked into the car and cut the roof right off. Calori was okay with that, and they continued to restyle the car. Herb took 3 inches off the top while Calori lowered the frame and installed a dropped axle. Other modifications followed, including swapping the engine out of his lakes racer that clocked 114.50 mph in 1948 at a Russetta meet.

Calori had cracked the door, and "How To Chop Your Top" was

Earl Bruce stands with his foot on the bumper of his customized 1939 Ford coupe outside of Big Top. Chopped by Jimmy Summers, the nosed and decked car featured deleted running boards, shaved handles, and filled rear side windows.

At the time, Barris's Custom Shop was located at 7674 Compton Ave. in Los Angeles. Note the misspelling in the advertisement of the inaugural issue of Hot Rod *magazine.*

Lou Baney stands proudly in front of his chopped 1932 5-window coupe. Running in the B Coupe class, Baney set the fastest time of the day at the November 1948 Russetta meet with a speed of 123.11 mph.

featured on the cover of *Hot Rod*'s October 1951 issue. Inside was a two-page story by Bob Pendergast that opened with the line, "One of the most oft asked questions received in the HRM mail is, 'How can I chop the top on my car?'" There are only two photographs and five sketches, and the copy greatly over simplifies the process (as I did above). However, that may have been all the incentive that the readers needed—it's easy; get 'er done.

The final paragraph cracked me up, "We wholeheartedly agree with Bob Rounthwaite [whose 3-inch-chopped 1934 3-window was featured in the same issue] that any amateur can do a decent chop job on a car if he knows his own limitations and distributes the necessary work accordingly."

By that time, the word was out, and Bob and Dick Pierson's heavily hammered coupe (9 inches) graced the cover of the April 1950 issue of *Hot Rod*. As *Hot Rod* predicted in its August 1948 feature on the Pierson's 1936 coupe, the new car was chopped significantly. Standing in front of the car, Bob Pierson made it look like a tiny Hot Wheels car.

The Piersons ran the car that August at Bonneville where they set two records: 149.005 mph with their own C-class engine and 146.365 with a B-class engine on loan from Bill Likes. In 1951, they ran the car with the Russetta Coupes Club. Speaking with Historian Greg Sharp, Bobby Meeks of Edelbrock said, "One of my

Some convertibles were chopped. They were easier to cut than a steel-topped sedan or coupe. This 1939 convertible sedan belonged to "Dode" Martin of Dragmaster fame. (Photo Courtesy Robert Genat Collection)

Glen Houser's Carson Top Shop was one of several shops in Los Angeles that specialized in padded and chopped tops as well as upholstery. The process was developed between 1935 and 1937.

jobs at Edelbrock was to find guys who could be successful racers and help them with the latest equipment."

After the Piersons agreed to prepare their coupe for the lakes, Meeks decided on the excessive roof chop.

"We were looking for high speed, and that dictated the narrow shape of the front end, the full belly pan, and the chop," Meeks said. "The rules said that the windshield had to be 7 inches high, but they didn't specify the angle. So, I laid the posts back until you almost lost vision (about 50 degrees) and then raised 'em up a bit—and that was it."

By 1951, when this photo of Howard Johansen's Howard's Cams Special was taken, chopped tops were abundant. In 1951, running in the B Modified Sedan class, the car reached a top speed of 131.964 mph at Bonneville. Later that year, at El Mirage, Howard went 148.29 mph with a 490-ci Marmon V-16.

The November 1949 issue of Hot Rod *included this photo of Gilbert "Gil" Ayala in his chopped 1940 coupe. Note the 1949 Cadillac rear fenders, the fadeaways, and the tape to keep out the El Mirage dust. On his first outing, Gil qualified at 127.11 mph. Opened in 1945, Gil's Auto Body Works was located at 4074 E. Olympic Blvd. in East Los Angeles.*

One of the few 1932 Tudors racing in the early days was Dean Moon's chopped sedan. Note the 18-inch rear milk-truck wheels and the pin-up girl grille insert. The car was later sponsored by Urick-Gibbs Motor Co, where Moon worked before he opened his own business. (Photo Courtesy Mooneyes)

With its patriotic red, white, and blue candy paint scheme, the Pierson Brothers coupe set the standard by which all other chopped coupes would be measured. It was the first car inducted into the Dry Lakes Hall of Fame.

Low was the way to go. In 1951, running alongside the Pierson Brothers coupe at Bonneville was what became the So-Cal coupe. Before it was the So-Cal coupe, it was the Oxnard, California-based chopped 1934 coupe of Jim Gray, Russell Lanthorne, and John Quinto (sans engine and transmission and finished in white primer). At the time, it wasn't as chopped as the Pierson Brothers coupe, but it would be, and it had a track nose by the legendary Indy car builder Frank Kurtis.

"Drag racing was really taking off, but it really had to be the right car," said Alex Xydias, the founder of the So-Cal Speed Shop. "I wanted a double-threat coupe—a car that I could drag race every Sunday and also run at Bonneville. I bought the Lanthorne-Gray coupe that had run a GMC 6 at Bonneville to a speed of 153.061 mph. Its top had been chopped to meet the SCTA rules that required 7 inches of windshield."

With the blown engine from Tom Cobb and "Buddy" Fox, the coupe was reworked at Cobb's Santa Monica shop in time for the 1953 Bonneville Nationals. Running in the C class with a 258-ci flathead set back 22 inches with a front-mounted 4-71 Jimmy blower and four Stromberg carburetors, the So-Cal team set a flying-mile record at 172.749 mph, wearing the #1 moniker on the door.

After the success of Bonneville, Cobb and Fox went their separate ways. However, Fox and Xydias continued to race the coupe at the drags, and they broke the existing record

with a run of 121.16 mph in the quarter-mile in the B class at Pomona. There was no doubt that the radically re-chopped, laid-back roof aided the aerodynamics. Next, came the addition of Ardun cylinder heads that enabled them to increase the terminal speed to 132.79 mph.

Xydias's brother-in-law, Dave DeLangton, who just returned from Korea, really wanted to drive and went 128 mph on his first pass. Sadly, on his next pass, the clutch let go, which cut some fuel lines and set the car on fire. On fire himself (a T-shirt was his only protection), DeLangton bailed while the car was still running out of control. Although he was rushed to the hospital, DeLangton suffered third-degree burns and died in the hospital four weeks later. For Xydias, the loss was too much, and he quit racing.

While radically chopped coupes, such as the Pierson and So-Cal coupes, were never the norm, they were certainly making an impact. In the wings was Compton's Chrisman clan (brothers Art and Lloyd and uncle Jack). The Chrismans had made a name for themselves racing the Harry Lewis–built Modified car that was made famous by LeRoy Neumayer at the Santa Ana Drags. Eventually, Neumayer sold the car to Art Chrisman. In Chrisman's hands, it became even more famous as the #25 car with flathead power and, later, Chrysler-Hemi power. It was the first dragster to reach 140 mph and was then the first dragster to reach 180 mph.

Built in the 1930s and upgraded continuously, the #25 car was getting long in the tooth to race competitively in the then-modern era. So, the Chrismans decided to build a new car specifically for Bonneville. Unlike most rods of the day that used a stock frame, the Chrismans opted for a lightweight, tube chassis that located the engine behind the driver, who

George Barris (front right) and his team at Barris Kustom Industries hold the recently separated roof from Larry Robbins's 1948 Mercury, which was fitted with an even newer 1949 Cadillac grille. Although George could and did wield the knife at times, his brother Sam did most of the bodywork. George handled the paintwork.

Restored by Roy Brizio Street Rods, Sam Barris's 1949 Mercury is on its way to be exhibited at the Wally Parks Museum. Besides the beautiful chop, this side profile shows how Sam removed the dog leg in the side and the downturn in the character line. Sam sold it almost as soon as it was finished.

was pushed scarily up against the radically chopped windshield.

The combination worked. In 1953, it arrived on the salt with three engines and the door gaps taped up. The first engine was a 304-ci Mercury out of the #25 car that set a one-way C-class record at 163.63 mph. Engine problems prevented a backup, so an Ardun-headed flathead was installed, and they set the B-class record at 160.187 mph.

The car appeared on the cover of the February 1954 issue of *Hot Rod* under the heading "The Most Fantastic Coupe!" In addition, at that year's Bonneville Nationals with Chrysler Hemi power, the Chrismans set the B-class record at 180.87 mph and the C-class record at 180.08 mph. The following year, running in the new D class, they set the record at a staggering 196 mph.

The car was eventually sold to George Barris, who famously and somewhat controversially reworked it for the television show *The Many Loves of Dobie Gillis*. Many people did not like this pearl-painted version with split doors, dragster wire wheels, and wheel spats, but its appearance on television influenced many viewers to tune in to the hot rod scene.

Ironically, all three of these iconic coupes (the Pierson Brothers coupe, the So-Cal coupe, and the Chrisman coupe) competed in the 2001 Pebble Beach Historic Concours d'Elegance's "Famous Hot Rod Coupes" class.

Things were hectic at Barris Kustom Industries when it was located at 11054 Atlantic Blvd. in Lynwood. The company produced this small, 5x8-inch, eight-page catalog. Sadly, there is no date on my copy.

DESIGNING

Barris

KUSTOM AUTOMOBILE
PRICE LIST

CONSTRUCTION

11054 ATLANTIC BLVD. LYNWOOD, CALIF. NE 6-4432 NE 8-5258

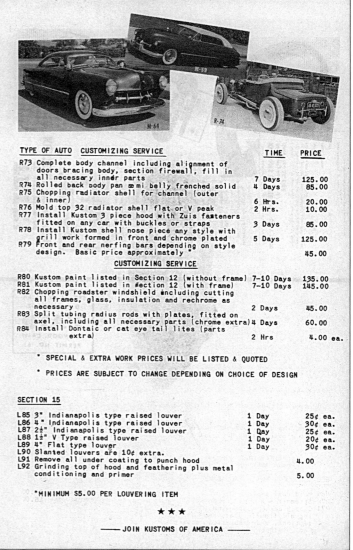

TYPE OF AUTO CUSTOMIZING SERVICE	TIME	PRICE
paper. Car is now completely cleaned and several color coats applied. The finished product includes detailing, cleaning and polish items etc.	4 Days	85.00
P57 Flaming or step off design in paint ir primer any color two tone flames with contrasting tips (on request) painted in lacquer or enamel, completely sanded primed and sprayed with 9 heavy coats.	8 Hrs.	25.00
P58 Stripping edges of flames and abstract design*	6 Hrs.	10.00

SECTION 13

	TIME	PRICE
M59 46-53 Ford and Merc. Chop convertible windshield and side windows, cut all glass plus rechrome all necessary parts and wind-wings	3 Days	130.00
M60 40-41 Ford Chop Conv. windshield, all glass windwings and rechrome necessary parts	3 Days	90.00
M61 36-39 Ford Chop. Conv windshield, all glass windwings and rechrome necessary parts	2 Days	60.00
M62 40-41 Chev. Chop Conv. windshield, all glass windwings and rechrome necessary parts	2 Days	90.00
M63 42-54 Chev. Chop Conv. windshield, all glass windwings and rechrome necessary parts		145.00
M64 Chop any hard top coupe with open windows, no side posts, special framing, chrome all necessary parts, complete top & side bracing, incl all glass & weather stripping incl. (Headliner extra)	3 weeks	650.00
M65 Chop any hard top coupe with rounded door posts, tapered Quarter panels, frenched drain molds, inc. all glass & etc. (Headliner extra)	3 weeks	600.00
M66 Chop standard model coupe with no restyle changes incl. all necessary material & labor for lowering top	3 weeks	500.00
M67 40-48 Ford & Merc Chopping top incl. same as in No. L-65	3 weeks	475.00
M68R emoving door post and install special framing		
M68 Removing door post and install special framing for glass same as No. L-64 But no chopping	2 weeks	300.00

* Any different work on side windows or changing styles of frames and glass, charged will be made accordingly.

SECTION 14   ROADSTER WORK

	TIME	PRICE
R69 Mold cowl vents	2 Days	30.00
R70 Streamline hinges, large roll	3 Hrs.	15.00 ea.
R71 Chop 3 early model window ford coupe (including all frames, glass body works, channel sections, and insulation rubbers)	7 Days	135.00
R72 Chop 5 window ford coupe (Same. as aboveL	9 days	150.00

TYPE OF AUTO CUSTOMIZING SERVICE	TIME	PRICE
R73 Complete body channel including alignment of doors bracing body, section firewall, fill in all necessary inner parts	7 Days	125.00
R74 Rolled back body pan semi belly frenched solid	4 Days	85.00
R75 Chopping radiator shell for channel (outer & inner)	6 Hrs.	20.00
R76 Mold top 32 radiator shell flat or V peak	2 Hrs.	10.00
R77 Install Kustom 3 piece hood with Zuis fasteners fitted on any car with buckles or straps	3 Days	85.00
R78 Install Kustom shell nose piece any style with grill work formed in front and chrome plated	5 Days	125.00
R79 Front and rear nerfing bars depending on style design. Basic price approximately *		45.00

CUSTOMIZING SERVICE

	TIME	PRICE
R80 Kustom paint listed in Section 12 (without frame)	7-10 Days	135.00
R81 Kustom paint listed in #ection 12 (with frame)	7-10 Days	145.00
R82 Chopping roadster windshield including cutting all frames, glass, insulation and rechrome as necessary	2 Days	45.00
R83 Split tubing radius rods with plates, fitted on axle, including all necessary parts (chrome extra)	4 Days	60.00
R84 Install Dontaic or cat eye tail lites (parts extra)	2 Hrs.	4.00 ea.

* SPECIAL & EXTRA WORK PRICES WILL BE LISTED & QUOTED

* PRICES ARE SUBJECT TO CHANGE DEPENDING ON CHOICE OF DESIGN

SECTION 15

	TIME	PRICE
L85 3" Indianapolis type raised louver	1 Day	25¢ ea.
L86 4 " Indianapolis type raised louver	1 Day	30¢ ea.
L87 2½" Indianapolis type raised louver	1 Day	25¢ ea.
L88 1½" V Type raised louver	1 Day	20¢ ea.
L89 4" Flat type louver	1 Day	30¢ ea.
L90 Slanted louvers are 10¢ extra.		
L91 Remove all under coating to punch hood		4.00
L92 Grinding top of hood and feathering plus metal conditioning and primer		5.00

*MINIMUM $5.00 PER LOUVERING ITEM

★ ★ ★

—— JOIN KUSTOMS OF AMERICA ——

Inside, the catalog copy stated, "There are no jobs too big or too small." Section 13 of the catalog listed chopping prices beginning at $475 for a 1940–1948 Ford or Mercury. Barris estimated the work to take three weeks.

What better way to tow your radically chopped 1934 Ford 3-window race car than behind a chopped 1936 3-window coupe. This photograph was taken by Don Cox at El Mirage, and it says all that you need to know about the attraction of not one but two chopped Pierson Brothers coupes. (Photo Courtesy Robert Genat Collection)

In 1989, Denny Kahler of Dublin, California, ran his chopped and custom Porsche 911 through the traps at Bonneville with an average speed of 220.615 mph.

Designer Fred Hidalgo built the Stink Bug in the late 1990s. It was one of the very first highboy bugs with a suicide I-beam axle hot rod front end. The chop was finalized by Lee Pratt.

In 2001, three coupes are shown in at Pebble Beach. The Pierson Brothers' 1934 coupe (front) is owned by Bruce Meyer, the So-Cal Coupe (middle) was owned by Don Orosco at the time, and the Chrisman coupe (last) was owned by Joe MacPherson at the time and was loaded with nitro.

This proved how important these cars were in the evolution of hot rods (and chopped rods in particular). Don Orosco won first place with his restoration of the So-Cal coupe, Bruce Meyer placed second with the restored Pierson Brothers coupe, and the Joe MacPherson–owned Chrisman coupe placed third. Art Chrisman had the last laugh, though, when he loaded the coupe engine and blasted the Pebble Beach crowd with eye-watering, nitro-laden fuel as he drove up onto the podium. It was a sight for sore eyes.

Of course, the Pierson Brothers, So-Cal, and Chrisman coupes were not the only chopped cars of the early, formative years of hot rodding. However, their radical cuts set the template and perhaps even the boundaries for all subsequent chops. It was amazing that the young rodders who performed these chops had no training in what they were doing, minimal reference from magazines, no use of the internet, very little experience, and few tools. It's amazing and is a testament to their tenacity that they performed such groundbreaking work—work that has influenced generations of hot rodders to continue to make the cut.

As you would expect, the majority of the cuts were made in the custom car, hot rod, and land speed racing worlds to the usual suspects: early Fords, Studebakers, and the occasional Porsche or Volkswagen.

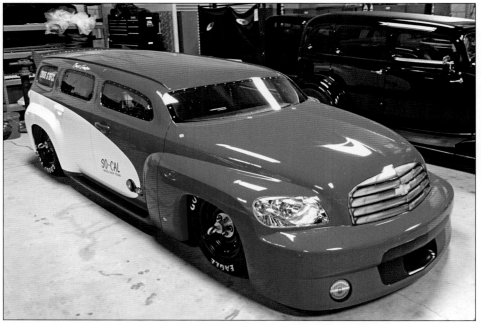

In 2005, Pete Chapouris's SO-CAL Speed Shop built this chopped four-door Chevy HHR to run at Bonneville, which it did in 2006.

Porsche? Yes. In August 1989, Denny Kahler of Dublin, California, ran his custom chopped 911 through the Bonneville traps with an average speed of 220.615 mph.

Sticking with the boxer brigade, Designer Fred Hidalgo purchased his sinister black Volkswagen Beetle already chopped, but it was poorly done, so he had Lee Pratt re-chop it. Because of their tapered greenhouse, VWs are hard to chop, but that doesn't stop people from doing it.

Returning to Bonneville, the Hudson Boys are a group of friends from Seattle, Washington, who have been racing there since 1968. The group has set (and holds) numerous records. Chopped by founding member Rich Thompson, a Geo Metro, which has been powered by various

Unfortunately, the Chevy HHR ended up on its roof at 249 mph after an engineer decided to change the attitude. Driver Jim Minneker walked away unharmed. (Photo Courtesy Randy Lorentzen)

Adrian Nassif's Model A coupe is also known as the Hoppin' Mad Rabbit. Nassif cut 10½ inches out of his Model A coupe that is also channeled over the frame. Note the "Traffic Violator" sign inside the passenger's side of the windshield.

Max Grundy and his buddy Justin Hill of Hills & Co. of Sydney, Australia, removed 3 inches from this 1961 Chrysler Newport, and it is so sleek that it looks as if it came like this from the factory. That is a compliment.

Suzuki motorcycle engines over the years, went 165 mph with a 1-liter engine and Janel Thompson behind the wheel.

In 2005, General Motors was working with Pete Chapouris's SO-CAL Speed Shop (written in uppercase to differentiate it from Alex Xydias' earlier So-Cal Speed Shop) to build a chopped four-door Chevrolet HHR for Bonneville. The 9-inch chop, complete with four opening doors, was performed by Bobby Walden at the SO-CAL Speed Shop, and it was a major piece of work. Unfortunately, the HHR flipped upside down at 249 mph in 2006. Thankfully, driver Jim Minneker walked away. The HHR was less fortunate, but it was eventually restored (but not raced) by Bruce Canepa.

In the hot rod world, there are guys such as Adrian Nassif (also known as the "Hoppin' Mad Rabbit"), who cut a whopping 10½ inches out of his Ford Model A coupe. Nassif and his well-hammered A-bone can often be seen racing at the various RPM Nationals West Coast events.

In the custom car world, no one is cutting it harder or finer that post-apocalyptic designer and car builder Max Grundy. Grundy first received mainstream attention when he was the resident artist for the annual Specialty Equipment Market Association (SEMA) Show. He goes where few have gone before when it comes to cutting up cars, as he has and continues to chop early 1960s Chryslers, including a 1961 Chrysler Newport two-door hardtop. "Hard-top" is the operative word here, as Grundy and Justin Hill of Hills & Co. Customs of Sydney, Australia, cut 3 inches out of the Newport while referencing a 3-D rendering by the Moffitt Brothers of Pea Ridge, Arkansas.

Grundy's maxed-out Mopar is stunning. It debuted to huge acclaim at the 2018 SEMA Show, and it proved that the chopping game is far from dead. In fact, we may have only just started. Hopefully, this book will inspire more people to make the cut.

If you're contemplating a chop and have never made the cut before, you can peruse the internet, where you will find lots of top chopping (in addition to reading this book, of course). As with all things on the internet, some content is accurate but other content is inaccurate. You just have to wade through it and choose what's right for you.

In addition, you can investigate metal-shaping classes. "The Secrets of Metal Shaping" is a three-day, hands-on class at Lazze Inc. in Grover Beach, California. At the time that this book was published, enrollment in the class was $1,790. Lazze Janssen is a Swedish metal shaper who has been shaping since 1996, and he teaches about 11 classes per year. The Tin Man's Garage Inc., another metal-shaping company, offers two-day classes for $1,200.

If you want something more specific than general metal-shaping classes, Joel Davis's Haus of Style is a good resource. At the time that this book was published, Davis's website (davishausofstyle.com) listed future two-day classes at $450, but I recommend checking with Davis before you make plans. Davis has hosted more than 50 classes that usually accommodate 16 to 20 people.

Beyond the knowledge that is contained in this book, tools (welding equipment and a selection of hammers, etc.) are needed, and they are dealt with in chapter 1.

Glass, of course, is the elephant in the room, and that is covered in chapter 17.

Top chopping is an art form, and it isn't for everyone, but with patience and care, it can be done, and it can be rewarding. Don't let anyone discourage you—have at it.

TOOLS AND EQUIPMENT

Top chopping does not require a vast number of tools. However, as with most bodywork tasks, it requires a welder (preferably a tungsten inert gas [TIG] welder for a precise weld), cut-off wheels (air or electric powered), an angle grinder, hammers, dollies, etc. You may also feel the need to acquire the skills to use an English wheel, and you can do so at a metal-shaping class. It's an acquired skill.

It's good to own your own tools, but ask yourself how often you will use them and if you will get a good return on the investment. Companies such as Baileigh Industrial have a "Used and Demo" section on their website that you can use to save some money. Baileigh is an international company and has facilities in Europe, Mexico, and Latin America.

We are extremely lucky in the US that tools and equipment are readily available and fairly reasonably priced. That is not always the case in other countries, where tools and equipment may be scarce and expensive. Of course, some of the tools can be acquired used, and if you only plan to chop one car, used tools are probably the smart way to go.

Frame-Up

Early top-chopping how-to articles, such as the one in the October 1951 issue of *Hot Rod* magazine, are interesting because they say little (and in *Hot Rod*'s case nothing) about supporting the body with a framework of steel tubing while you are chopping. Obviously, the technique of supporting the body after the roof has been removed is a method that has evolved as more people have learned more about chopping.

In my visits to numerous shops, there is no tried-and-true method for building the support structure. Some folks use the minimum number of tubes to tie the body from side to side and from the front to the back, and some seem to go overboard. With that being said, of all of the shops that I visited and the chops that I photographed, none compare to Rick "Speed" Lefever's shop in Pomona, California.

Lefever has been around race cars all his life, as his father raced in NASCAR. After school, Lefever became a fabricator at the renowned SRD race shop in Malvern, Pennsylvania, regularly working on cars for racers such as Bill Jenkins, Frank Iaconio, and Richie Zul. In Lefever's world, there is only one way that's the right way. Luckily, I was able to follow Lefever as he worked on a chopped 1930 Ford Model

A coupe for his son Rayce.

Lefever began with a massive adjustable fixture that was fabricated from 1½x3-inch steel. It has movable crossbeams as well as adjustable uprights to support the drivetrain and the body. With this fixture, every aspect of the build can be leveled and plumbed to perfection—or, as close to as you can get with an old Ford. (For more information about this rack and build, see chapter 3.)

Not everyone goes to the extreme that Lefever does, but he's a professional race-car builder who cuts no corners. Other builders may not be quite so exacting, but that doesn't take anything away from their efforts, which can produce equally good results and perhaps do so on a tighter budget than Lefever's.

For example, renowned metal shaper and fabricator Bobby Walden inserts turn buckles into his support structure so that he can make finite adjustments to the body to make it exactly square. Do you need to do that? Your answer depends on how precise you want the finished job. If you're not too worried about precise measurements, don't worry. However, if you want the finished car to be square, do all that you can to make it so. ∎

Frame-Up CONTINUED

If you are a professional car builder, a frame fixture (such as this adjustable one built from 1½x3-inch steel by Rick "Speed" Lefever) is invaluable. Note the moveable crossbars and adjustable uprights.

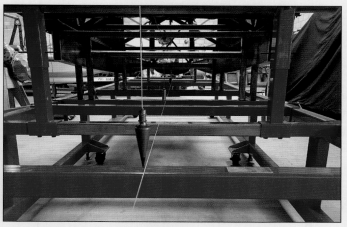

Looking through the middle of the fixture with the car's frame and body in place, you can easily see Lefever's center line and the various plumb bobs hanging.

This photo of a 5-window coupe that was about to get cut was taken at SO-CAL Speed Shop more than 20 years ago. It shows that a good support structure was deemed necessary even at that point in time.

Metal shaper and fabricator Bobby Walden uses hardware-store turn buckles to make easy and accurate alignment adjustments.

Bobby Walden's turn-buckle method offers infinite alignment adjustments when getting the body square before and after the roof is cut.

Because he has chopped the top of hundreds of cars, Jay Kennedy knows that he can often get away with using a minimum of support, but a ratchet strap is often good for pulling the A-pillars inward.

An angle grinder can be the top chopper's best friend. It is valuable for grinding, sanding, and even cutting with the use of different accessories, such as a cut-off wheel. My Hitachi G10SR has been reliable.

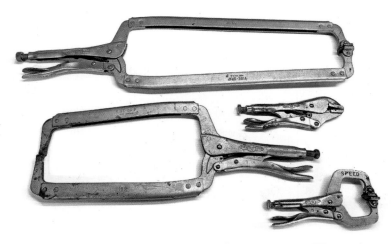

Vice-Grips (also known as locking pliers) are essential for chopping tops, and you will need several of them. Unfortunately, if you are not a full-time body man, you likely won't know exactly which ones you need until you need them. They are available in many shapes and sizes at a variety of price points.

Many professional body and metal workers use Cleco fasteners to hold the panels that they are working on in position. You might think that they are unnecessary, but once you get used to using them, they become extremely valuable. Cleco kits are available from a wide range of suppliers, including Eastwood, Summit Racing Equipment, and even Walmart.

Some auto-body workers say that the material from a cut-off wheel can contaminate the metal, but we're only on this planet for a short while, so I'm not sure that it matters. These are air-powered cut-off wheels, but if you do not have access to air, many electric and cordless options are available.

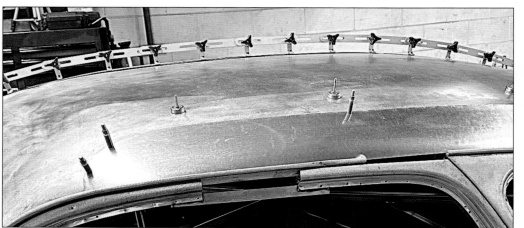

Mike Wagner at Cornfield Customs specializes in metalwork and likes to use these adjustable contour gauges. They are available from companies such as Eastwood for less than $100.

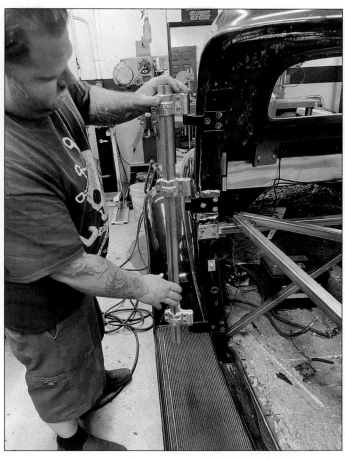

This Hinge-O-Liner, which is available from Thomas Kearney's Leading Edge Machine & Design, is being used at Troy Ladd's Hollywood Hot Rods. Its adjustable design provides precise hinge alignment.

Dykem layout fluid is available in blue and red from many suppliers and welding shops. It helps to reduce glare so that you can see your scribe marks more easily. Dykem also makes marker pens, which can be handy. A 12-ounce aerosol can costs about $20.

A bullseye pick is a tricky tool to master, but once you learn how to use it, it can be used to remove dents or make metal straight quickly and accurately in blind areas. Bullseye picks are available in various throat sizes (typically from 15 to 30 inches). They are available for about $100 or more from a number of sources, such as Collision Services, Trick Tools, and US Auto Supply.

Sawzall is a registered trademark of Milwaukee tools, and it is the term that is often used to describe any brand of reciprocating saw. A reciprocating saw works well to cut the sheet metal of the top and the wooden support structure (if there is such). This type of saw is available from many suppliers, and blades are available for cutting metal or for cutting wood.

Not everyone uses sheet-metal skin wedges (also known as pry bars or pry tools) because you can improvise by using a different tool if necessary. However, these simple tools work well to align panels before welding. They are available for about $30 each from numerous outlets, including Metal Magery, which also sells other tools and specialty fasteners.

For general-purpose welding, I use this Miller Dynasty 200 tungsten inert gas (TIG) welder. It can be used to make precise welds when joining mild steel, aluminum, or stainless steel. TIG welding is a two-handed process (one hand holds the torch while the other feeds filler metal), and it commonly involves a foot pedal or fingertip remote to control the arc voltage while welding. As with metal inert gas (MIG) welding, a shielding gas (typically argon) is required.

I've had great luck over the years with the Ridgid brand wet/dry shop vacuum. However, I recently replaced a large 16-gallon, 5-hp version with a smaller 9-gallon, 4.25-hp version. In this case, size does matter. I should have kept the 5-hp version.

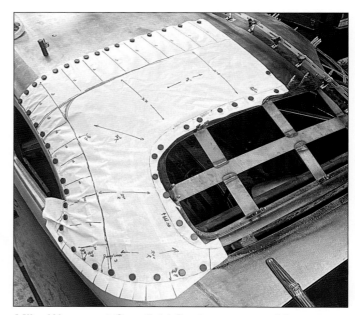

Mike Wagner at Cornfield Customs uses white auto body masking paper to make his templates. Other builders use brown paper or cardboard. It really doesn't matter what your preference is—as long as it works for you. The paper is available in various widths from 3M or any good body shop supplier.

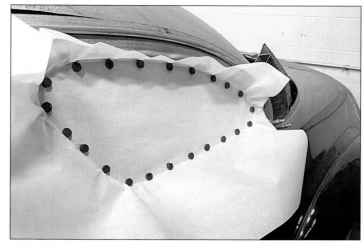

Most metal shapers have a huge selection of hammers and dollies, but Rick Lefever only uses these. Some of these tools can be found at garage sales, swap meets, and on the internet. Eastwood offers a seven-piece set that is made in the USA. For about $255, the hammer and dolly set includes three hammers; toe, heel, and general-purpose blocks; and a light dinging spoon.

Mike Wagner at Cornfield Customs uses these small round magnets to hold his template paper in position. Magnets are a handy addition to any metal shaper's tool box, and they are usually reasonably priced.

Bobby Walden of Walden Speed Shop works with Baileigh Industrial. Here, he uses Baileigh Industrial's English wheel (also known as a wheeling machine), which is used to form compound curves from flat material. The process is not easy. It's a skill that is developed over time. The price of new wheels varies greatly from about $1,500 to $10,000 for the heavy-duty professional option. Then, of course, you will need all the attachments. Wheels can sometimes be found used, but they are generally sold quickly.

FORD MODEL TS

In the early days of hot rodding (before World War II), Ford's Model T dominated the oval-track motorsports scene. However, the majority of those who competed on California's dry lakes used cut-down Ford Model T roadsters that had minimal equipment to reduce weight and go fast. Coupes and sedans, with their tall, flat-screen facades, were rarely raced. Since open-top cars were available for bargain prices, why would anyone race a coupe or sedan?

With the postwar boom in hot rodding paired with the general acceptance of coupes and sedans that was pioneered by the Russetta Timing Association and the Valley Timing Association, competitors began to race cars other than roadsters. One of the wackiest race cars to hit the lakes was Guy "Red" Wilson's massively chopped 1925 Ford Model T sedan. Cut a staggering 14 inches, the car was also lowered 6 inches. To quote the caption in *Hot Rod Handbook*, "This permits a minimum of wind resistance and a maximum of hurry."

The car also featured a track nose (seen on the cover of the May 1950 issue of *Hot Rod* magazine) that Wilson borrowed from his track roadster.

"Red was the one who added the cigar to the Clay Smith Woody Woodpecker logo because he and Clay both had red hair and smoked stogies," said American Hot Rod Foundation historian Jim Miller. "Red married Clay's wife after he died and took over running the company. They also both worked at Bill Stroppe's."

Wilson's sedan eventually ended up in the hands of Chet Herbert, who raced it with Frank and Jim DuBont with Herbert's 298-ci 6-cylinder GMC engine and a Wayne Horning head. In July 1951, racing at a Russetta American Racing Club event, the *Beast*, which now had a slightly more aerodynamic nose, went 135.33 mph. The driver sat with his legs in the nose and his face pressed up against the windscreen.

Also racing a cut-down Ford Model T at the Northern California drags and the lakes in 1951 was Gene "Windy" Winfield. Winfield raced the *Thing*, which was a channeled 1926 Ford Model T with a dramatically raked windscreen. At Bonneville in 1951, Winfield had a best top speed of 134.932 mph with 247-ci flathead Mercury V-8 power.

There were other Ford Model T coupe and sedan racers—but not many. Ford Model As and 1932 models

may have been heavier, but they were far more aerodynamic. Of course, many racers continued to use Model T roadster bodies, especially for many Modifieds and Track Roadsters.

Fast-forward to the modern era, and class rules no longer apply, which leaves the Model T ripe for interpretation. For example, take the *Penny Hemi* 1927 Model T coupe on Model A rails. Owned by Alex Carlos, the bad-to-the-bone *Penny Hemi* is powered by a 1956 354-ci Hemi with a Weiand log intake and six Stromberg carburetors, and he built the car in a two-car garage.

Tim Dempsey's 1927 Ford coupe was done in a similar but even more radical vein. Dempsey owns Dempsey Kustoms in Des Plaines, Illinois, and his drag-inspired coupe *Twisted Sister* is powered by a GMC 6-71-blown, 327-ci, small-block 1962 Corvette engine that is fed by four Stromberg carburetors. There was never a 1927 Ford 3-window coupe, so Tim hand-formed his own around an original cowl and a sectioned 1954 Chevy dash.

With young enthusiasts, such as Carlos and Dempsey, carrying the Model T flag, the chopped Model T may live onward for another 100 years. We can only hope.

Guy "Red" Wilson, who earned the nickname because of his red hair, stands tall beside this radical, B-class 1925 sedan that was chopped 14 inches. With the engine in the back, Wilson's legs in the nose of the car, and his face pressed up against the windscreen, Wilson reached a top speed of 127.62 mph. (Photo Courtesy American Hot Rod Foundation)

The nose of Wilson's Model T was borrowed from his track roadster that Ed Cassold drove in California Roadster Association events and crashed. The roadster was on the cover of the May 1950 issue of Hot Rod. (Photo Courtesy American Hot Rod Foundation)

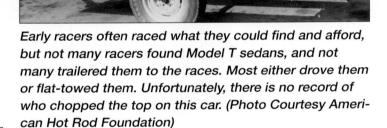

Early racers often raced what they could find and afford, but not many racers found Model T sedans, and not many trailered them to the races. Most either drove them or flat-towed them. Unfortunately, there is no record of who chopped the top on this car. (Photo Courtesy American Hot Rod Foundation)

Hammering down the concrete at Santa Ana, the Gene Thurman, Bob Herzog, and, later, Fred Voigt creation was made from a 1927 Model T body that was mounted on a Model A frame. It thrashed the Pierson Brothers' coupe with a speed of 142 mph.

In 1951, the Model T sedan was in the hands of brothers Frank and Jim DuBont as well as Chet Herbert. The car was aptly named the Beast—as were Herbert's motorcycles and later race cars. The Model T sedan was powered by Herbert's 298-ci Jimmy, and with that aerodynamic shovel nose in place of the track nose, it managed a top speed of 135.33 mph at the July 1951 meet.

At Bonneville in 1951, Gene Winfield's 1927 Model T, which was known as the Thing, ran in the Modified Coupe class. The Thing was powered by a flathead engine and reached a top speed of 135 mph. Although it is now gone, Winfield built a tribute car that was complete with purple paint and an aluminum nose.

Alex Carlos's Penny Hemi *can often be seen competing at West Coast events, such as the Race of Gentlemen Flabob Airport Drags. That 6-pack-equipped 354 engine can haul. The tuck 'n' roll top matches the white firewall that Carlos fabricated.*

As Ford never made a 3-window Model T coupe body, Tim Dempsey decided to fabricate his own around an original Model T firewall. The Drag-style T is powered by a Jimmy-blown, 327-ci small-block Chevy from a Corvette.

Sherry Martin's Chevy-powered Model T Tudor features a bamboo top and is shown during the Race of Gentlemen Flabob Airstrip Drags. However, a wooden top is not conducive to racing.

RICK AND RAYCE LEFEVER: FORD MODEL A

It's not always easy growing up in the shadow of a talented fabricator, such as Rick Lefever, but Rick's son Rayce seems to bear the burden well and spends his spare time learning fabrication skills when he's not playing the saxophone. For a few years now, this father-and-son team has been working on the weekends on Rayce's 1931 Ford Model A coupe.

The story really began in 1973, when a young Rick Lefever went to see the movie *American Graffiti*. The film had a huge effect on Rick, as it did many kids, and Rick immediately began building his own version of character John Milner's 1932 Deuce coupe. At just 13 years old, Rick didn't have much money, so in place of Milner's car, he focused his energy on a 1931 Model A coupe that he found in an old barn in the Amish hills of Pennsylvania.

Being a racer, Rick's Chevy-powered Model A had wheelie bars, long ladder bars, race-inspired graphics, wide N50x15 Pro Trac tires, and front and rear fiberglass fenders. However, it didn't have a chopped top. It was something that he prom-ised himself he would do one day. He raced it all over the Northeast, and it ran 10.80 ETs in the quarter mile.

Fast-forward to today. Rick is a meticulous fabricator, and before any bodywork was started on Rayce's project, Rick had the body acid dipped to give them as clean of a starting point as possible while identifying any issues. For example, the bottom body bead had rusted through in several places and needed patching, as did the areas at the bottom of the cowl and the bottom of the body behind the doors. There was lead, rust, and poor previous repairs, but there was nothing that couldn't be fixed.

After the body was back from the dippers, Rick mounted it onto his homemade frame table that he used to accurately locate mechanical components, such as the rear end, transmission, and engine, using an alignment bar of 2-inch steel tubing. Most builders do not go to this extreme, but Rick is a renowned chassis builder who has worked on dozens of race cars—he knows what he's doing, and he does it right.

After the mechanical compo-nents were set up on the table, the body was installed. However, as you can see from the photographs, the specifications changed and continue to do so. For example, in the setup shots, Rick and Rayce intended to complete a conventional build with a small-block Chevy, Turbo 400 transmission and a 9-inch Ford rear end. Along the way, that combination was canned, and the new powerplant was a supercharged Ford Coyote with a G-Force 5-speed manual transmission turned on its side. The 9-inch rear end was retained.

To support all of this, Rayce and Rick were going to build a tube frame. However, they reconsidered and tried a pair of bobbed Deuce rails from SO-CAL Speed Shop. Then, they finally decided to build a full-tube, race-style chassis after all. Unfortunately, they were not very far along when this book was printed. Nevertheless, I captured the roof chop that Rick wasn't able to execute for his teenage build.

"I just didn't know enough as a teenager to know how to do that." Rick said.

Rayce Lefever's 1931 Model A coupe is shown after it returned from the dipper. Note the bracing in the front cowl and inside the body. In addition, note all of the small parts hanging inside the car as well as the rusted-out lower body bead (particularly on the cowl).

Rick Lefever's race-ready 1931 Model A coupe was built when he was only 13 years old. Note the ladder bars. Fenders were must-have items at the time.

Rayce worked with his father, Rick, on this project. Here, Rayce uses a cordless drill to enlarge the holes in the body after removing the striker panel.

Rayce cleans the parts that he previously removed from the body. Always wear eye protection.

Rick has a precise eye for detail. This is his homemade, adjustable frame table. Note how the intended rear end, the transmission, and a mock-up plastic small-block Chevy are mounted on a 2-inch-diameter alignment bar.

Next, Rick mocked up the body, which was straight from the dipper, along with a particle-board mock-up wheel/tire to show how everything will eventually align.

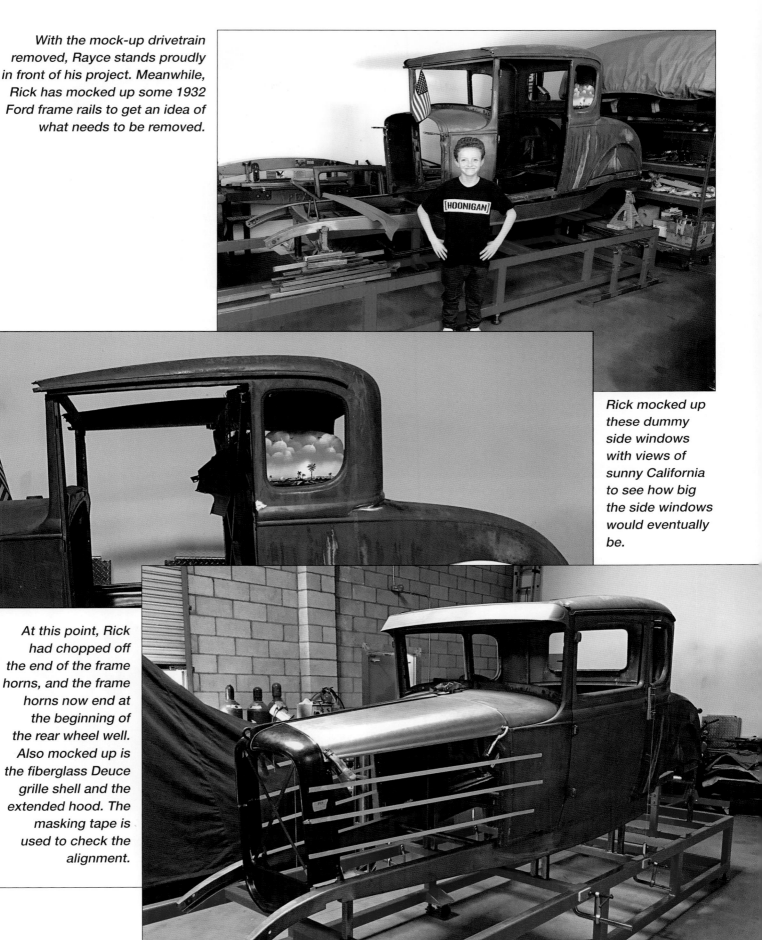

With the mock-up drivetrain removed, Rayce stands proudly in front of his project. Meanwhile, Rick has mocked up some 1932 Ford frame rails to get an idea of what needs to be removed.

Rick mocked up these dummy side windows with views of sunny California to see how big the side windows would eventually be.

At this point, Rick had chopped off the end of the frame horns, and the frame horns now end at the beginning of the rear wheel well. Also mocked up is the fiberglass Deuce grille shell and the extended hood. The masking tape is used to check the alignment.

Rayce's Model A coupe was squared on his father's frame fixture. A center line can be seen that runs from the front to the back, and plumb bobs are dropped down before measurements are taken to confirm squareness. Note the digital level.

This view shows how extensive Rick's body bracing is.

The bracing that was used while the body went for dipping has been removed, and extensive bracing using 1-inch square steel tubing has been installed farther back to keep the body square.

Rayce uses an air-powered cut-off wheel to slice through the Model A's A-pillars. Care and protective eyewear are essential.

This photo shows four things: 1) The frame rails have been bobbed to align with the bottom of the rear wheel well, 2) the marking for the cut is on the back of the roof, 3) the area where the back window will be lowered is shown, and 4) the top half of the A-pillar has been removed.

The problem with dipping a body is that you are likely to uncover more than you bargained for. In this case, it revealed bad repairs, rust, and vintage lead that must be removed and repaired.

On the driver's side, Rick performed the necessary repairs. He removed the rust and the lead and repaired the areas that were previously poorly repaired.

This shows how Rick intends to lower the rear window. He cut both sides of the opening and then across the bottom, just above the reveal.

The rear part of the roof on the driver's side shows where Rick intended to make his horizontal cuts. Note that the plan was to remove 5 inches from the vertical height.

There's not much steel left, so Rayce and Rick were easily able to lift what was left of the roof away from the body.

Using the predetermined cut lines that were marked into the Dykem, Rayce uses an air-powered cut-off wheel to slice through the back of the roof, being careful to follow the line.

After cutting through the upper line, Rayce shifts his attention to the lower line and carefully makes the second cut.

After the cut lines were cleaned of any burrs and irregularities, Rayce and Rick put the roof back on to make sure that it aligned and was square.

This close-up of the back of the roof shows where Rick had tack welded the rear window back into position and how the roof is clamped into position. Note that the big gaps will be adjusted as the roof is positioned correctly.

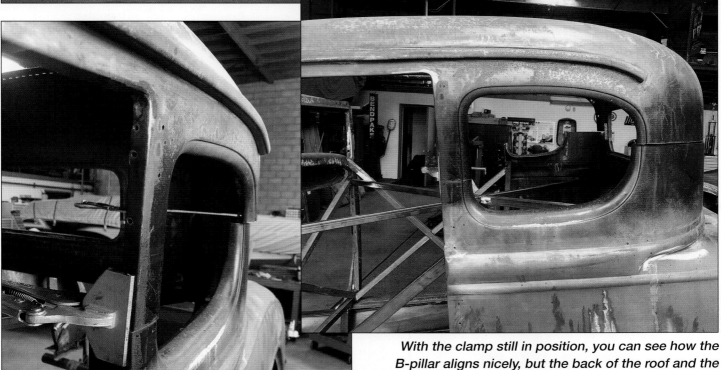

With the clamp still in position, you can see how the B-pillar aligns nicely, but the back of the roof and the shape of the window opening need massaging.

With the B-pillar clamped into alignment, the rear corner of the roof is out of alignment by approximately a half inch. However, that can be maneuvered to align.

Rick clamps the A-pillars into position. Thankfully, because the Model A top is fairly square, alignment is not much of a problem.

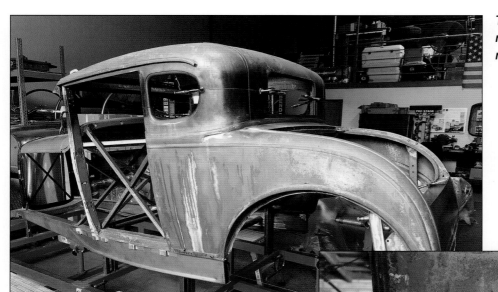

The view from the rear shows that the rear of the roof aligns and that the rear windows retain a nice shape.

This is the view from inside the cab looking at the rear of the roof on the passenger's side. Note that the top of the rear window frame has merely been lapped over the lower part of the body. That will be addressed.

Rick has removed the rear upper quarters of the roof along with the overlap shown above. On a Model A, these panels are bolted together, and the seam is disguised with the beading.

This shows how the upper rear corner of the roof has been pushed out to align with the lower part of the body. Note that there is a tapered gap to be filled with sheet metal.

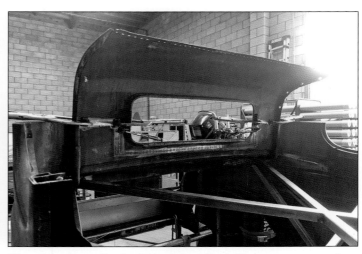

The view from the inside shows that Rick uses several body clamps to hold everything in position before he does any tack welding.

The big gap is comprised of the area on each side of where the body was originally bolted together. Rick removed the flanges and will eventually fill the gap.

With some pushing, pulling, hammering, and welding, the top begins to align with the body. You can see where Rick tacked it into position.

On the passenger's side, the top rear corner has been removed prior to being massaged into shape.

This is the bolt-on top rear corner after it had been removed and shaped slightly to align with the body.

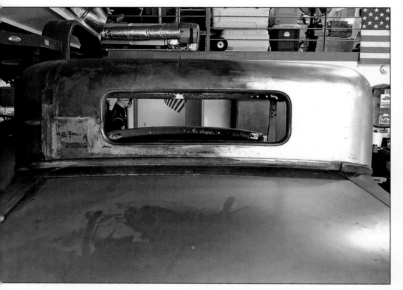

The finished passenger's side is shown. Work on the driver's side includes the tapered gusset that was needed when the seam was removed.

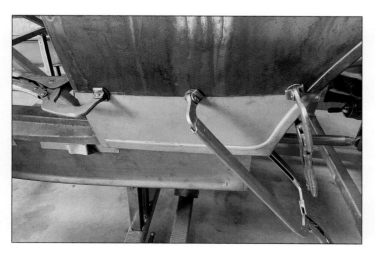

Rick meticulously metal finished the passenger-side rear corner. There is no longer a seam where the top bolted together.

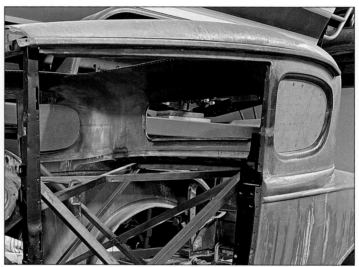

After the top was welded into position, Rick installed these wooden templates that he made earlier to make sure that both window openings were exactly the same.

With the top nearing completion, Rick turned his attention to the lower quarters of the body that were rusted out. New patch panels were obtained from John Reid.

From inside the body, you can see where Rick carefully stitched in and hammer welded the patch panels.

Attention was turned to the roof, where Rick plans to install an orange acrylic insert. So, this steel panel was rolled up and its curvature was checked. It will be used as a form for the acrylic.

Pieces were fabricated with a step in them for the thickness of the acrylic and then curved to fit the Model A roof.

After the insert frame had been welded, Rick inserted it into the roof, using Clecos to hold it in position.

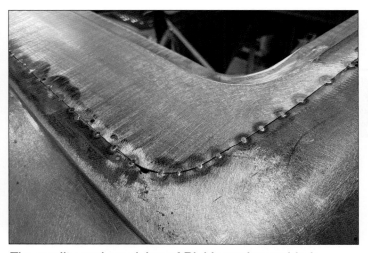

The insert receiver frame has now been stitch welded into position, and the Clecos have been removed.

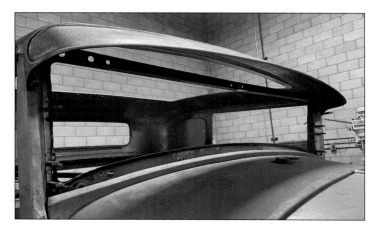

The quality and precision of Rick's workmanship is shown. Eventually, he'll go back and hammer weld the whole seam.

A new sun visor was obtained. However, as usual, Rick couldn't leave well enough alone, as it was too reworked to meet the aesthetic that he wanted.

This is what the car looked like when this book was sent to the press. The Coyote engine, which will be supercharged, is pushed back under the cowl.

VEAZIE BROS. FABRICATION: BRUCE FORTIE'S 1932 FORD 3-WINDOW COUPE

Aside from the 1933–1934 Ford Model 40, it is likely that more 1932 Ford 3-window coupes have been chopped than any other car. They're just asking for it like a dog waiting to play fetch with a stick. Bruce Fortie's Brookville Ford 3-window coupe is no dog—far from it—but he felt that it needed a few inches out of the top. So, he took it along to Evin and Justin Veazie of Veazie Bros. Fabrication in Pomona, California.

Bruce Fortie's Brookville 3-window coupe is shown before the chop at Evin and Justin Veazie's hot rod fabrication shop in Pomona, California. The hood was louvered by Jimmy Shine, and under it is a stack-injected 392 Hemi engine.

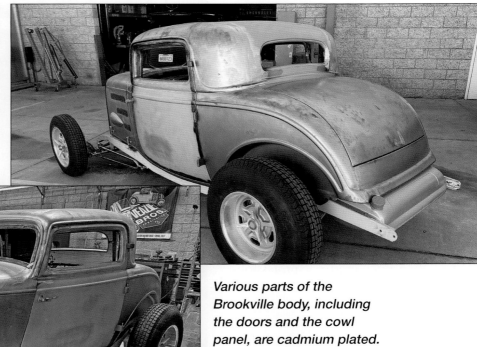

Various parts of the Brookville body, including the doors and the cowl panel, are cadmium plated. I wondered if this would have an effect on the welding, but it didn't seem to be a problem.

Chopping the Top

The Veazie brothers worked for the late Pete Chapouris at the famed SO-CAL Speed Shop and worked on a number of SO-CAL builds, including the Lindig's Indy Speedster that won the 2012 America's Most Beautiful Roadster Award. After Chapouris died, the brothers began operating in one of the vacated SO-CAL buildings. However, despite their well-earned credentials, they had never chopped a top before this one. With that being said, they did an excellent job with the tricky task.

Before attempting any roof chop, do some research. That's exactly what Evin and Justin did before they jumped into Fortie's project. Evin called the nearby Kennedy Brothers, Jimmy Shine, and others for advice, and, as you would expect, he received many answers. The only certainties for the project were to carefully plan the work, dive into the deep end, and remember to measure twice and cut once.

Before any cutting was done, the body needed to be braced. In this case, the car was a brand-new Brookville 3-window that one would expect to be square, which, of course, it was. However, if you are chopping an original body that may have been repaired more than once (and not professionally), check the body for squareness.

Do this by bolting the body to a frame that you know is square or to a frame fixture or table. Next, before measuring to make sure that the body is square, hang some plumb bobs (preferably three): one at the front, one in the center, and one at the rear of the body. If it's not square, some pushing

The Veazies used a large amount of 1-inch square steel tubing to brace Fortie's cab. Doing this is a lot of work, especially for something that will be removed from the finished product. However, it's necessary, and the tubing can be salvaged for future projects.

Extensive bracing is shown under the front cowl. Longitudinal braces run from the front to the back, and cross-braces tie them together.

and pulling will need to be done to get it into shape. There is no point in proceeding with the chop until you have the body square.

Once you have the body square, begin to brace it. Most people, Evin included, use 1-inch square steel tubing to hold the body together when the roof is removed. The body has a tendency to spring apart, so it is necessary to tie it together front to rear, side to side, and diagonally. As with the actual act of chopping the top, there are many ways to install the bracing, and it doesn't really matter *how* you do it—as long as you do it.

Don't underestimate the work that is involved in bracing, particularly if you use turnbuckles to facilitate some adjustment. That is particularly useful on an old body that is possibly out of square and needs some adjustment.

Even after some extensive bracing, Evin discovered that he had mounted the cross-brace from the bottom of the door to the cowl too high, so that had to be moved down. Of course, he could salvage the tubing and use it for another project.

Once the bracing was complete, Evin carefully planned his cuts and decided to take a simple geometric approach to cut the roof in a step that allowed him to remove 2 inches and lower the top until it aligned with the body.

For his first attempt, it was an amazingly smooth operation that took less than an eight-hour day to complete. Note that this was the roof chop only (not the doors, the garnish moldings, or all of the small bits). However, it did include the front posts that, because of their inner structures, are somewhat finicky.

With the roof surprisingly easily cut in just one day, Evin moved on to

Initially, these diagonal braces ran from the bottom rear of the door opening and went up diagonally to the A-pillar (above the latch mechanism). However, they got in the way of the part of the A-pillar that needed to be worked on.

the doors, moldings, etc. The doors proved to be relatively simple because there are only two, there are no wind wings, and the rear B-pillar is almost vertical. There is some internal structure to the posts that needs to be addressed and some woodwork that must be done, but it's not too complicated if you have made it this far.

After cutting the doors, Evin moved on to the inner door-window garnish moldings, the rear window garnish molding, and the front screen inner moldings. The front screen inner moldings were somewhat tricky to complete, but, by now, Evin was getting the hang of it. Finally, he cut the front windshield, which was not difficult to cut because of its simple construction.

Considering that he had never chopped a car before, Evin did a great job and executed perhaps one of the best (and certainly cleanest) 2-inch chops that I have seen. In addition, he did the major part of a chop in just one day.

Fabricator Greg Hirata adjusts the diagonal door brace by moving it below the latch mechanism so that it doesn't interfere with work that is needed on the A-pillar.

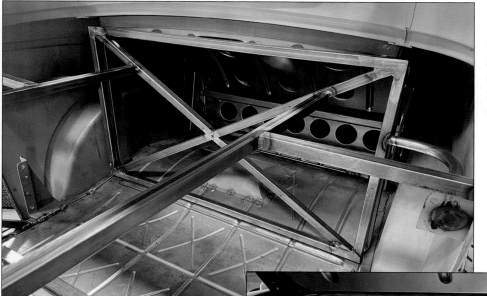

This is the rear bracing that Evin Veazie installed behind the doors of Fortie's 3-window coupe. The longitudinal braces are anchored to a rectangular frame. That rectangular frame is cross-braced and anchored to the floor and the body sides.

Looking into Fortie's 3-window coupe through the trunk and up to the firewall, you can see how the rectangular frame in the back is cross-braced and tied to the front cowl.

When chopping a top, it is important to measure twice and cut once. Here, Evin made a number of scribes in the Dykem before he finally figured out his cut lines.

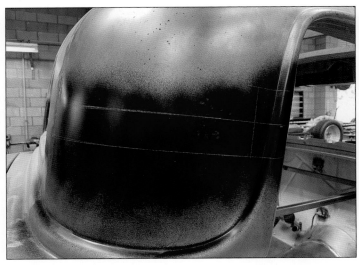

This is where the 2-inch cuts were originally planned. However, Evin decided to take a different line and cut the roof lower, down near the roof-to-body swage line.

Evin planned to cut the A-pillars in the middle where the pillar is straight. However, the folded-steel inner structure within the pillar requires some careful working so that you don't break your cutting tool.

After Evin made up his mind where the cut was going to be, he used 1/4-inch blue tape to mark his cut line. You can see below the tape where the curved cut will be.

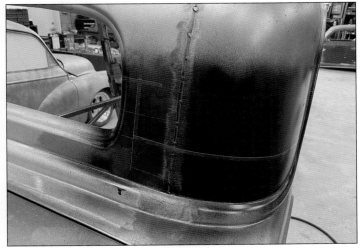

Meanwhile, at the back of the roof, the tape continues. Notice how the cut is square and that the roof, after it has been cut, will drop down. Just as planned, it aligned well with the body.

Evin uses an air-powered cut-off wheel, but you could use a cordless drill or, worse, an angle grinder if that's what you have. You could use a reciprocating saw, but if you're not careful, you could bend the metal.

Evin makes the vertical cut along the rear window. He always wears protective eye wear because a hot spark in the eye is not fun.

Evin moved on to the vertical cut behind the doorjamb. Some people say that cut-off wheels contaminate the metal—and they may. However, does it really matter? How else can you make such a precise cut?

After the vertical cut was made, Evin cut the door post. Remember, there is support structure in the post, so care is required in this area.

The first cut is the deepest. Ignore all of the scribe lines except the curved one at the bottom near the roof-to-body swage line. That will be the 2 inches that are eventually removed.

Evin uses a cut-off wheel to slice through the outer skin of the A-pillar. Remember to be careful in this area due to the folded sheet-metal inner structure.

After completing the cut, four people lift the roof off the body. However, you could always tie the car's roof to the roof of your shop or a gantry crane and roll the body and frame out from underneath.

Evin and his brother Justin place the upturned roof onto a sturdy portable workstand. Notice how the stand is wrapped with bubble wrap to protect the roof from accidental damage.

It is clear to see where the cuts were made. Thankfully, the rear part of the body is single-skinned and not at all difficult to cut with a cut-off wheel.

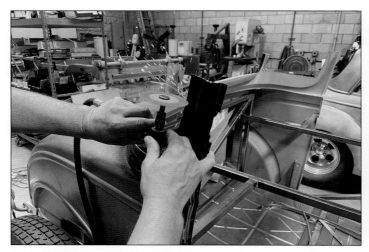

Using the cut-off wheel, Evin removes a 2-inch section from the rear doorframe. If you don't have a cut-off wheel, you could use an angle grinder or even a hacksaw if that's what you have.

The blue tape indicates where Evin is going to remove the 2 inches. Notice how the cut line follows the roof-to-body swage line. This is a good way to do a 2-inch chop.

Evin follows the tape carefully with the cut-off wheel. Remember, the more care you take, the less clean-up work is required when the roof and body are reunited.

Evin makes the curved cut in the rear. This was done carefully with the cut-off wheel. You can also see him cutting the rear window frame.

This view of the driver's side from inside the body shows the curved cut. Again, precise use of the cut-off wheel gets the job done.

At this point, the A-pillar has yet to have the 2 inches removed, but the trickle of Dykem that has run down the post indicates that extra work will be necessary in this area to make the cut invisible.

Because of the multilayered inner structure, Evin used a reciprocating saw to remove 2 inches from the A-pillar. Of course, he could have used a cut-off wheel, but he felt that the reciprocating saw was better suited for the task.

The structure that Ford used to strengthen the A-pillar is shown. Be attentive when cutting this so that you don't break your saw blade or cutting wheel.

Evin and Justin discuss how the lower part of the A-pillar will be reworked to disguise the chop and make it look like it did from the factory. In the end, they followed the swage line between the A-pillar and the cowl.

Owner Bruce Fortie holds the roof steady while Evin uses a pair of tin snips to cut the curve into the panel behind the door. This aligns with the curve cut into the body.

It took a few people to lift the roof back onto the body. Evin and Justin fudge it into position to see how it aligns with the body now that 2 inches have been removed. It's actually not very far out of alignment.

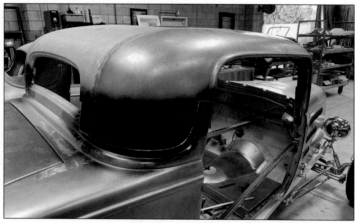

With the roof merely balanced on top of the body, you can see that this clean and simple approach resulted in a very clean joint with no need for splits in the roof. A 3- or 4-inch chop might have been different, though.

Evin uses a block of 2 x 3 wood to support the top and to make sure that he is giving the car enough windshield. Most States, such as Iowa require the minimum vertical height of the unobstructed windshield glass to be 6 inches, which is the length of a dollar bill.

You can see just how close the roof and the body align even after the 2-inch section was removed. After some pushing and pulling, it's time for some welding.

From the inside, Evin marks where he has to remove some metal so that the top aligns better with the body. You can see from the crack that it's close.

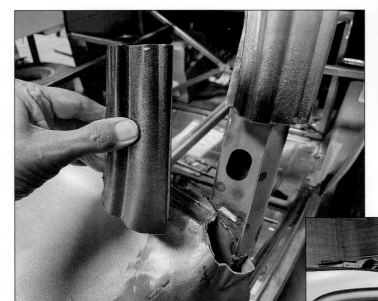

After removing the lower portion of the A-pillar, you can see the inner structure. Some planning was needed here before any further cuts were made so that mistakes were not made.

Even uses an air-powered grinding wheel to adjust the inner structure of the A-pillar. You could use an angle grinder if you don't have compressed air.

There is some misalignment between the upper and lower parts of the A-pillar, but that will be fixed. Evin cuts carefully into the bottom of the A-pillar (where it joins the cowl) with a reciprocating saw.

The lower portion of the A-pillar was sliced until it fit back in the hole. There's a little misalignment but nothing that a bit of welding won't cure.

After the A-pillar's inner structure was resolved, Evin began TIG welding the pieces back together. The beauty of steel is that you can just add and grind until you get it right.

Greg "Portapower" Hirata lends a hand (two, actually) to align the top of the A-pillar with the bottom while Evin tacks the inner structure into position. Hirata isn't putting stress on the pillar, he is just holding it in place.

After the inner structure was fully welded, the front face of the A-pillar was shortened to fit the gap. As you can see, it's a snug fit, and weld will fill any gaps.

Using his TIG welder, Evin carefully tacked the front of the A-pillar into position. If you don't have access to a TIG welder, just about any welder will do the job.

After the A-pillars were tacked into position, Evin moved to the back on the passenger's side and stitched the roof into position. Note how he tacked every half inch or so.

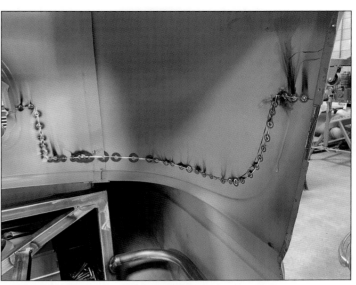

This view from inside the cab shows the driver's side and the reverse view of Evin's tack job. Notice that no splits were made in the roof to make it align with the body.

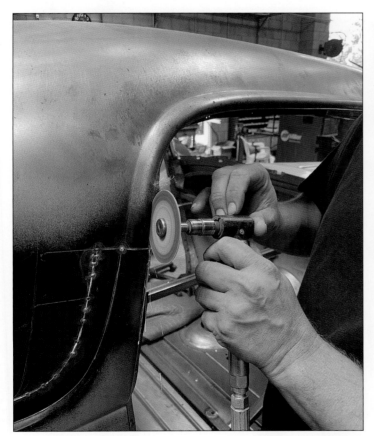

Moving back to the rear doorjamb, the top doesn't align perfectly with the bottom because of the missing 2 inches. Evin used a cut-off wheel to slice the doorjamb just after the turn.

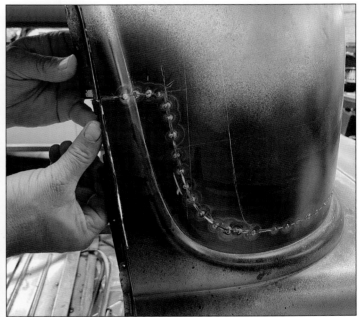

This is where he sliced up the jamb so that the top could be aligned with the bottom. The top is pulled out just a fraction of an inch to align with the bottom.

Evin uses an 8-inch sheet-metal clamp to secure the doorjamb flange. If you don't have one of these clamps, any method of clamping will suffice.

With the sheet-metal clamp holding the parts in alignment, Evin uses the TIG welder to tack everything into position.

With the clamp removed, you can see how Evin tacked the length of the split after aligning the top and the bottom. He'll go back and finish weld it later.

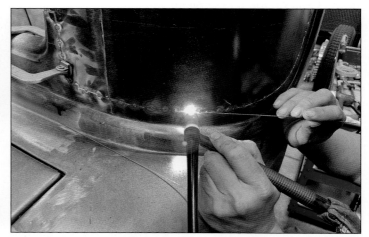

Moving from spot to spot to minimize distortion, Evin TIG welds the joint. He welds just an inch or so of material at a time.

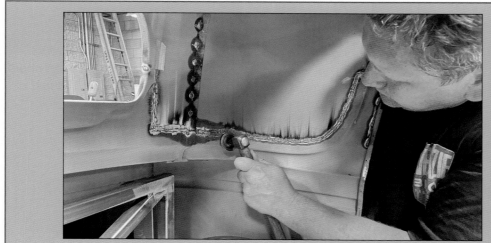

With a hammer and dolly (on the outside of the panel) Evin hammer welds the seam. This hammering of a tack weld (or a welded joint) while it is still hot flattens the joint and releases tension.

After the joint was welded and hammered, the whole area was ground smooth. Be careful not to scuff it too vigorously, though, because you'll only have to put more work into finishing it later.

The main area has been sanded smooth, and you can barely see where the pieces join. This has to be one of the neatest chops that I have ever seen, and it is something that almost anyone could tackle with minimal skills.

Chopping the Doors

Thankfully, chopping the doors of a 1932 3-window is a reasonably simple process because the top is not too tapered. Therefore, the A-pillars are not too raked, there are no wind wings, the window does not have that little fillet at the back (like the Model 40), and there are only two of them.

Of course, there is some inner structure to deal with, and despite what Ford said, there is an oak support structure above and behind the doorjamb that requires some woodworking. Likewise, there is wood around the rear window, and wood was used to support the rear window mechanism. However, there's nothing too demanding.

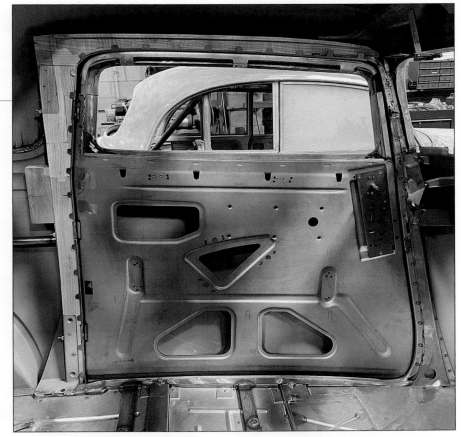

Ford advertised that its bodies contained no wood, but that wasn't actually true. The 1932 coupe had an oak structure across the top and behind the doors to support the hinges.

Evin removed the wood from around the doors and cut and glued the wooden structure using a stepped joint until it matched his chop.

It's nice to work with brand-new steel (even if it is galvanized, as the doors are), and TIG welding it proved to be no problem.

This shows where Evin made his cuts to the door: about 1 inch above the top hinge and at an angle down into the reveal at the A-pillar.

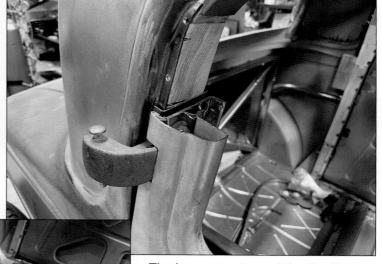

The inner structure of the B-pillar just above the top hinge is shown. Thankfully, it's reasonably straight in that area.

The front end of the door at the A-pillar has a little more inner structure, but you can only weld what you can reach. Don't stress over it.

After carefully measuring and making his cuts, Evin tacked the top of the window frame back onto the door.

Evin used a magnetic welding holder, which is available from companies such as Chicago Electric Welding, to hold the door in position.

At the top of the A-pillar, Evin made two pie cuts to reshape the corner. For his first effort, it came out well.

This close-up of the B-pillar shows not only where the doorframe was cut but also how the two halves almost align.

The same can be seen at the front A-pillar, where Evin's pie cutting has the edge of the door almost in line with only minimal cleanup.

From the backside of the doorframe, you can see where Evin began to piece the frame back together using small pieces of sheet metal.

Inside the doorjamb, Evin cut away the support structure when he made the pie cuts to the frame.

With the door supported on a steel welding bench, Evin began the task of TIG welding all of the previously tacked joints.

This shows how Evin stitched the inner doorframe back together. Welding and grinding will finish it up.

Evin added a small bead of weld to the door edge that can be built up and ground down until the shape is perfect.

After all of the welding has been completed, Evin cleans up the welded area with an air-powered orbital sander.

Welded and sanded, the inner doorframe looks almost as good as new with only minimal signs of work having been done.

All of the finish work was performed on the steel welding bench, and the door is now ready for installation. The three hinges were retained.

The door almost looks like it did from the factory when it is closed. There is a little gap at the top, but as you can see, it still needs adjusting.

Bits and Pieces and Garnish Moldings

Compared to the work that was previously completed, chopping the inner window garnish moldings to match the doors is not difficult. The rear was easy because the sides are almost vertical. However, the front needed some finagling.

Thankfully, finishing off the chop on a 1932 3-window coupe is not extremely difficult because there are only three windows and not many garnish moldings, and due to the way that they are constructed, they are not too difficult to section. It just takes time and patience to get it right, make it fit, and get it to look as if Henry Ford intended it to be that way.

If you have a car that is missing some of these moldings or they are too rusty to use, they are available new from suppliers such as Brookville Roadster, CW Moss, and United Pacific. Fiberglass window garnish moldings are also available, but the fit might not be as good as you'd hope.

The wood that frames the top and rear of the door may be rotted away. New wood is available from companies such as FordWoodArt .com.

This is the backside of one of the inner window garnish moldings. It was a simple construction, and it's not difficult to cut.

After being sectioned, the rear of the passenger-side inner molding was tacked into position. There is some misalignment.

The front corner of the driver-side molding was mitered and tacked into place. Making the cuts as neat as possible will help.

The inner molding is fitted to the passenger-side door, where there is a bigger gap to be filled—but nothing drastic.

On the driver's side, you can see that chopping the inner moldings to match the doors was not overly complicated.

Finish welded and sanded smooth, the inner molding on the driver-side door is finished, and you cannot see that it was cut.

The chopped passenger door and its respective inner molding are ready to be installed back on the car.

Due to its two-piece construction, the rear window's inner molding was actually the easiest of all the moldings to modify.

The oak structure behind the door is covered with a steel striker jamb. The wood and the jamb are available new.

The striker jamb is easily sectioned above the top hinge, although a little judicious welding and fudging is necessary.

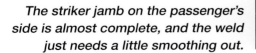

The striker jamb on the passenger's side is almost complete, and the weld just needs a little smoothing out.

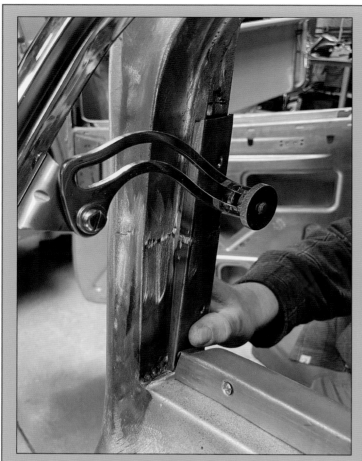

The windshield garnish moldings are simple but slightly tapered. Similar to the window moldings, they need fudging as necessary.

Welded, fudged, and ground smooth, the sectioned windshield garnish molding looks as good as Ford's original.

There are no garnish moldings on the A-pillar doorjamb, so it's just a matter of welding and grinding until the jamb is smooth.

THE KENNEDY BROTHERS: TWO 1932 FORD 3-WINDOW COUPES AND A 1932 FORD 5-WINDOW COUPE

It's possible that no one has chopped more hot rods than Jay Kennedy of the Kennedy Brothers Bomb Factory in Pomona, California. Jay has chopped dozens of cars—from Ford Model A pickups to coupes and sedans. Nothing appears to faze him, and he takes it all in stride.

During many recent visits, I caught up with Jay as he was chopping Dick Wade's Ford 3-window coupe. The coupe was a nice, original hot rod that only needed 3 inches to be removed from the top, and Jay followed the tried-and-true method of leaning the A-pillars back and pie-cutting the front of the roof to pull out the top of the pillars.

At the same time, Jay was also reworking Tom Busch's coupe, which had been chopped 3 inches at a different shop. Unfortunately, the chop on Busch's coupe was not executed very well (as could be seen by the inside welds), and the top had some tension. Jay relieved the tension by slicing across the roof, toward the insert, about two-thirds of the way back. The top immediately sprang apart about 1 inch. Although the gap was only about 1 inch, Jay elected to remove a larger slice and insert a piece about 3 inches wide.

Of course, the window frames were now too short, and because Jay had not done the original chop, he had no left-over material to use to extend the frames. Instead, he had to make the window-frame structure. It's a complicated piece of origami that requires some dexterity to form and install.

Now that they have been finished, Wade's and Busch's Ford 3-window coupes have different profiles, and you can decide which version that you prefer: vertical posts or laid-back posts. Neither option is wrong.

Thanks to Jay, I also had access to his photos of a 5-window coupe that he had chopped. I was hoping that it would be the "Devil Deuce" chop, but it was not. It was the chop of Jim Butler's car. The chop was perfectly executed. It's interesting to note that the 3-window coupe has three door hinges because of the length and weight of the doors, whereas 5-window coupe doors only have two hinges. In addition, the 5-window coupe has a rain gutter, whereas the 3-window coupe does not. Two hinges make for an easier chop, as does the lack of a rain gutter.

Dick Wade's 1932 Ford 3-Window Coupe

This photo was taken at the Kennedy Brothers Bomb Factory in Pomona, California, and it's apparent that the top of the 1932 3-window coupe's A-pillars are fairly vertical. They lean back slightly, but the rear of the roof is quite straight. The door posts lean inward, but, with everything considered, it's not a bad shape to cut.

The doors were removed along with the inner wood structure and the striker doorjambs. For the moment, a single piece of angle iron holds the body apart, but more support structure will be added.

The back of the roof has already been chopped and is semi-finished. The panels that were removed have been stitched back in.

This is out of sequence, but you can see the square-tube structure that Jay built to support the body. In addition, there is a faint white line on the roof where it will be split.

Removing 3 inches of material caused some misalignment in the A-pillars. However, Jay raked the bottom part of the pillar to regain the alignment.

Inside the rear corner of the passenger's side, you can see how the corner was reinstalled as well as the two horizontal splits going toward the rear window.

Inside the rear corner of the driver's side, the corner is partway welded in with some stitching on the far right. There is still a lot of work to do.

On the outside, the driver's side was hammer welded and mostly ground down. Notice how Jay welds in short, 1-inch bursts so that the metal does not distort.

The rear of the roof on the passenger's side is now finished and smoothed out. You can barely see where the pieces joined.

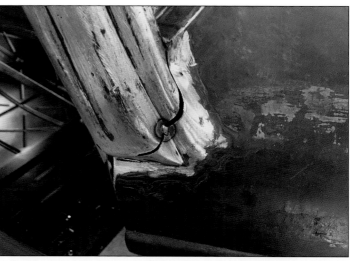

To rake the A-pillars, Jay made this cut from the corner of the windshield down to the swage line at the bottom of the post.

To be able to pull out the top of the windshield to align it with the bottom of the post, Jay made this narrow pie cut in the roof.

On the driver's side, you can see the lower cut and how the post was pulled back to align with the A-pillar.

This close-up of the front corner of the roof shows how Jay inserted a small slice of steel to fill the pie cut that was tacked into place.

Expanded, this view shows not only the lower portion of the A-pillar but also the pie cut in the roof that has now been welded closed.

Jay finished welding the passenger-side A-pillar and began to grind it smooth. Still, there is some finish work to do.

This photo was taken partway through the welding process after Jay had welded the passenger-side A-pillar. The driver's side A-pillar still needs to be completed.

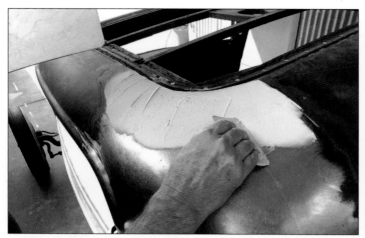

Jay turned the coupe over to his brother Joe, who used filler where necessary. In this case, it was used around the rear corner of the roof insert.

The passenger-side A-pillar was shaped, smoothed, and given a protective coat of paint.

After the filler work was completed, Joe gave the area a coat of black primer to protect it.

Wade's 3-window coupe is partway through the finishing process with the windshield in place.

This is Wade's coupe before it was chopped. Note that the three door hinges were retained, whereas some chops only employ two.

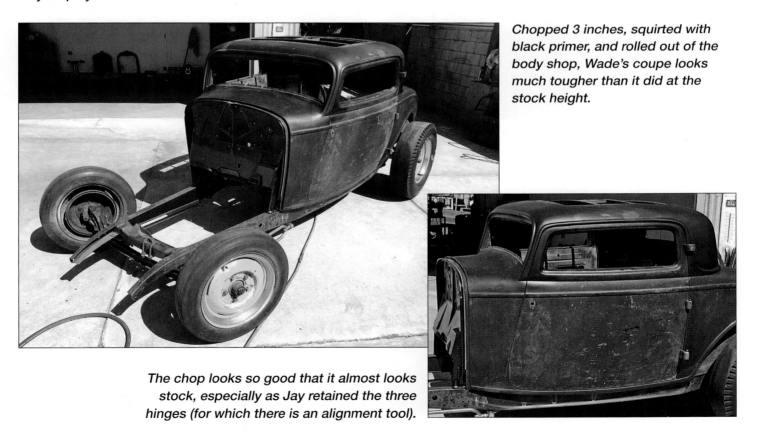

Chopped 3 inches, squirted with black primer, and rolled out of the body shop, Wade's coupe looks much tougher than it did at the stock height.

The chop looks so good that it almost looks stock, especially as Jay retained the three hinges (for which there is an alignment tool).

Tom Busch's 1932 Ford 3-Window Coupe

Tom Busch's 3-window coupe was chopped without leaning back the posts and without stretching the roof, which was under some tension.

Using a reciprocating saw, Jay cut the roof about two-thirds of the way back, and it sprung apart about 1 inch, showing how much tension that it was under.

A view inside the body on the passenger's side shows just how rough the chop was. There was plenty of welding, hammering, and filling.

The driver's side looks much the same, but Busch decided not to ask Jay to go there. However, the door wood needs lengthening.

Rather than just filling the missing inch, Jay cut and folded some sheet metal about 3 inches wide and inserted that into the roof.

Because the roof is now longer than it was at the beginning, the door tops required lengthening to match. This is the inner structure of the door post.

Jay retained the top hinge and cut the window frame just 1/4 inch above the hinge before the doorframe curved to match the roof.

Because Busch's coupe was chopped previously, the stamped-steel doorjamb striker did not need any work.

Jay cut the original door tops and separated them before folding up some sheet metal to fill the gap that was created by lengthening them to match the roof.

Of course, the front of the door required a little reworking to make it align, but this was not a difficult task.

Jay uses a body hammer and dolly to carefully shape the metal insert that was previously cut to fill the gap in the door top.

Forming the insert is a tricky task unless you have access to a spare doorframe from which you can cut a piece.

Comparing Ford 3-Window Coupe Chops

I was lucky enough to capture Wade's coupe (foreground) and Busch's coupe as they were being chopped and re-chopped by Jay Kennedy. The difference in the A-pillar angles is clear.

Jay leaned back the posts on Wade's 3-window coupe, but on Busch's car, which previously was chopped, the A-pillars are more vertical.

From the rear, it is apparent that the two methods of chopping resulted in rear windows of different shapes and sizes. Wade's car has a slightly larger rear window. Neither method is wrong.

From the front, it's difficult to see how the posts differ, and neither version is wrong. However, I prefer Wade's leaned-back posts.

From this low angle, the two 3-inch chops look about the same. It's only in the side profile that you can see the difference between raked and non-raked A-pillars.

Ready to go home, Wade's chopped 3-window coupe is typical of the work coming out of the Kennedy Brothers' Pomona shop, where they build nice, traditional, no-frills hot rods.

Kennedy Brothers Ford 5-Window Coupe

This very nice, rust-free 5-window coupe came into the Kennedy Brothers Bomb Factory for a 3-inch chop. Notice how the 5-window coupe has rain gutters and two door hinges, whereas the 3-window coupe has three hinges and no gutter.

After all of the hardware was removed, Jay taped out his first cut line on the passenger's door. Notice how he chose the most vertical part of the B-pillar for his cut line.

On the passenger's side, you can see where the initial taped cut line is repeated. In addition, a small wedge was inserted into the door gap to keep it consistent.

The top is gone. Jay made his cuts in three different places where the metal aligns. In addition, he removed the outer metal of the A-pillars.

The roof was put back onto the car, tacked at the B-pillar, and tacked at the back of the rear side windows. Some misalignment is visible around the back.

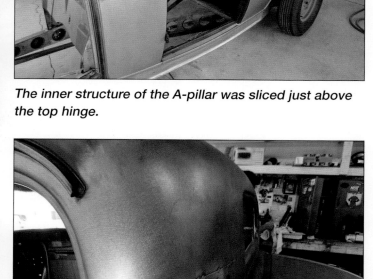

The inner structure of the A-pillar was sliced just above the top hinge.

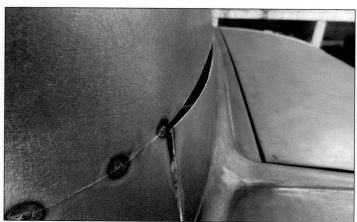

The back of the roof was gradually massaged back into alignment just by judicious pushing and pulling.

A few steps further on in the process, Jay pushed the back of the roof into position and tack welded the various splits together.

The joint in the inner structure of the A-pillar is about an inch or so above the hinge.

Jay removed the complete outer sheet metal of the A-pillar instead of cutting it in the middle. This results in a cleaner A-pillar.

On the driver's side, it is visible where the outer sheet metal of the A-pillar was reinstalled, providing a nice, clean line.

The outer sheet metal of the passenger-side A-pillar has yet to be reinstalled.

The outer skin of the passenger-side A-pillar was tacked into position. Note the split at the top of the pillar to facilitate alignment.

At this point, the outer sheet metal of the passenger-side A-pillar was finish welded and ground smooth along with the split in the top of the pillar.

The passenger-side B-pillar was finish welded and ground smooth. However, the back of the roof remains tacked and not yet finish welded.

Apart from a little hammer welding and smoothing around the back, the main part of the chop is now complete.

After Jay completed the main portion of the top chop, he turned his attention to the doors and cut off the tops.

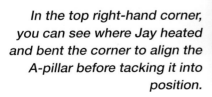

In the top right-hand corner, you can see where Jay heated and bent the corner to align the A-pillar before tacking it into position.

The clean lines of the A-pillars are significant. They were achieved by removing and reinstalling the outer sheet metal without cutting it.

Although there is still some finishing to do at the back, Jay's chop of this 5-window coupe was clean, and the leaned-back posts just look right.

With only 2 inches removed, Jim Butler's 5-window coupe looks almost stock—or how it perhaps should have looked from the factory.

WALDEN SPEED SHOP: 1932 FORD 5-WINDOW COUPE

There are various approaches to chopping a top, and none are wrong as long as the final result is pleasing to the eye. Bobby Walden of Walden Speed Shop in Pomona, California, has been moving metal for longer than he cares to remember, and he is renowned for his steel roof inserts, door skins, and metal-shaping classes. His philosophy is to cut the doors first and then make the roof fit the doors. It's not wrong; it's just different.

"The reason I chop the doors first is to nail the door window profile, which, in my opinion, defines the top chop," Walden said. "If you look at the *California Kid* or the *Vern Luce Coupe*, it's the chop profile that makes the car look good from the side. The side profile, which is the door window opening, determines the angle of the roof, which determines if the chop is aggressive or not."

I caught up with Walden when he was performing a 3½-inch chop on a brand-new 1932 5-window coupe from United Pacific Industries (UPI) for customer Joe Pickford. While UPI no longer supplies assembled bodies, it does produce all of the component

panels if you need to replace a part or panel or if you feel bold enough to attempt assembling your own.

Unlike a lot of metal-shapers, Walden is meticulous and tends to use sturdy fixtures, make templates, and use more measurements than the rest of us before he makes a cut.

There's nothing wrong with that, as is evidenced by Pickford's finished 5-window coupe that was featured in *Wheel Hub* magazine.

In addition to his renowned metal-shaping classes, Walden has videos of his chops that you can view on his website and YouTube channel.

This isn't the car that Bobby Walden is chopping. However, it's an example of an all-new 5-window coupe from United Pacific Industries (UPI). Assembled bodies are no longer available, but UPI manufactures all of the panels and hardware.

This is Joe Pickford's 5-window coupe as it arrived to get its top chopped at Walden Speed Shop in Pomona, California. Notice the sturdy fixture structure that Walden uses when assembling bodies from component panels.

UPI also supplies the rear and rear side window structures as well as all of the relevant hardware, such as striker posts and hinge posts. This is helpful, especially if you're rebuilding a basket case.

When they were available assembled, the UPI bodies were complete from the direct-replacement floor up to the ash (hardwood) roof bows.

The top was not initially welded together. Instead, it was held together with sheet-metal screws. It was due to come apart.

As mentioned in the introduction, unlike everyone else, Walden cuts the doors first and then makes the roof fit. It's not wrong; it's just different.

The door on the right was already chopped. Walden likes to make wooden templates for the windows so that they are exactly the same.

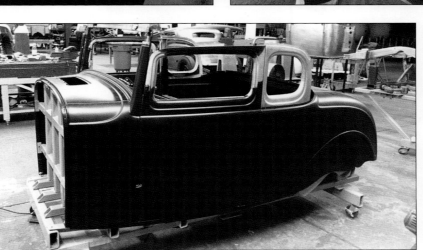

You can see at the top and the bottom of the front of the window frame how the frame will require some additional material.

On the driver's side, Walden checks how the panel will get attached to the lower body and how the window is going to fit.

The windshield posts remain un-chopped with the inner header panel in place, but the chopped doors were hung to see how it looks.

From the passenger's side, the cowl seam that needs to be welded later is even more obvious. The fitment of the doors is good.

At this point, the body was removed from the assembly fixture and installed on one of Walden's signature Deuce frames.

Switching to the passenger's side, Walden clamped the already-chopped rear side window-frame panel to the lower body.

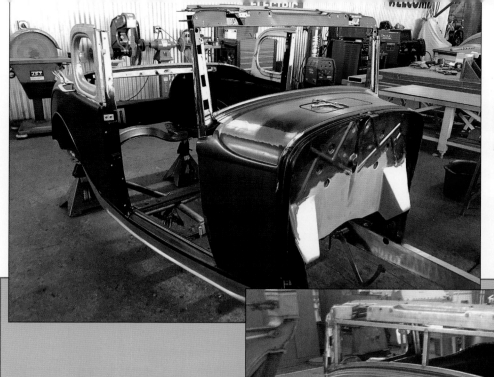

Walden is working on the rear side windows. The front windshield remains uncut at this point.

Walden cut the A-pillars, and the body is back on the assembly fixture. The cowl seam was welded, and there's a fixture for the windshield posts.

Just as he did for the doors and the rear side windows, Walden made a wooden template for the rear window, indicating a 3½-inch chop.

With the roof on his bench, Walden cut out the rear window, sectioned it 3½ inches, and welded it back into position.

After the rear window was complete, Walden slipped the roof back on to see how it looked and to determine where he would make the necessary cuts.

The stitch welding can be seen every inch or so around the rear side window and the back of the top before Walden went back to complete the welding.

The top was installed and finish welded, and the cowl seams were finish welded.

The top was finish welded and ground smooth. The rear side windows were also finish welded and ground smooth. Note that the gutter was installed.

This is not something that you can easily try at home. However, to reach certain areas that need to be welded and to install some of the wood, Walden upended the body.

No seams are visible on the inside of the roof at the rear because Walden never made any cuts there. Of course, the wood had to be sectioned.

UPI uses ash hardwood for all of the inner structure. It is a good resource if your wood is missing or rotten.

The wood had to be sectioned, and the inner window garnish molding had to be sectioned to match the window openings.

Getting ready for paint, Joe Pickford's chopped 5-window looks perfect with its blown small-block Chevy engine. Note the filled roof.

You would never know that this is a brand-new body and not original Henry Ford steel. Notice how the cowl vent and the four-piece hood were retained.

Finished, painted, and on the road, Joe Pickford's 5-window coupe looks stunning—from its curved rear spreader bar to its spindle-mount Halibrand wheels.

HOLLYWOOD HOT RODS: 1933 FORD 3-WINDOW COUPE

Henry Ford loathed annual model changes. His beloved Model T endured for almost 20 years (from 1908 through 1927), but his competitors were pushing the envelope and technical advancements, which was something that had to be done. The Model A, which was the Model T's replacement, was almost outdated before it was introduced at the end of 1927. Hot on the heels of the Model A came the Model B and, more importantly, the Model 18, which featured Ford's groundbreaking mono-block V-8.

Eventually, the V-8 set the world on fire, but the body on which it rode was short-lived, leading to annual styling changes for Ford. Introduced at the end of March 1932, the 1932 Ford was quickly replaced by the Model 40, which was designed by Eugene "Bob" Gregorie and Edsel Ford. Gregorie joined Ford in 1931, working in the aircraft division. However, as Ford drifted away from aviation, Gregorie moved over to the automobile division and went on to establish Ford's first styling department in 1935.

"The tractor, car, or truck went through this stage of making small-scale models," said Charles Sorensen, who was Ford's head of production and the father of the production line. "Then, when one was finally decided upon, a full-scale model would be built."

The styling cues of the 1933 Model 40 can be seen on the full-size clay model of the 1932 Ford that was photographed in October 1931. While the grille of clay was not overly attractive, it was swept out at the bottom. Soon after, early in 1932, the tiny Model Y, which was destined for the United Kingdom (UK), was unveiled, and it displayed the delicately curved grille that would be increased in size for the Model 40.

Built on a 112-inch-wheelbase chassis (6 inches longer than the 1932 model), the 1933 Model 40 was a stylish car and enjoyed an improved V-8. It now had aluminum cylinder heads that allowed a compression increase from 5.5:1 to 6.3:1 and featured a horsepower increase from 65 to 75. Sadly, the 1933 Model 40 was short-lived and only a few more than 300,000 were built before Ford introduced the 1934 version.

The 1934 Model 40 is essentially the same car as the 1933 model. However, the grille lost its curve and a few bars, and the chrome surround became fatter. The hood sides had straight (rather than curved) louvers and two handles (rather than one). Nevertheless, it remained a stylish car, and as America crawled out of the Great Depression, about 564,000 were built.

This particular 1933 3-window coupe belongs to Dan O'Connell. It went to be chopped at Troy Ladd's Hollywood Hot Rods, where Kyle Connole handled most of the work and Marcio Luz and Geoff Wheeless were involved in the finishing work. Something that I had not seen before was the Hinge-O-Liner kit from Thomas Kearney's Leading Edge Machine & Design in Windsor, Colorado. Beautifully made, the Hinge-O-Liner is available for several applications, and it certainly makes hinge alignment a cinch when chopping or restoring old cars. At the time that this book was published, prices began at $375.

Following along as Connole and the others chopped O'Connell's car was quite an eye opener. Connole has his own methods that work for him, including rarely wearing eye protection unless he's welding. While it works for him, it's not something that I recommend. However, he has performed dozens of top chops—and the results speak for themselves.

This 1933 3-window coupe was found by Dan O'Connell on the internet and brought to Troy Ladd's Hollywood Hot Rods in Burbank, California. It sits along-side Darren Houck's bare-metal 1934 coupe that was already chopped. O'Connell liked the chop on Houck's car, and Kyle Connole used it is a template for the cut.

Using 1-inch square steel tubing, Connole fabricated this simple support structure that holds the car together after the roof is removed. Most importantly, the support structure secures the cowl to the back of the cab.

The Model 40's suicide doors have three hinges from the factory, but Ladd and Connole decided that O'Connell's car would look better if they eliminated the top hinge and moved the middle hinge upward to be in the center of the beltline.

HOW TO CHOP TOPS

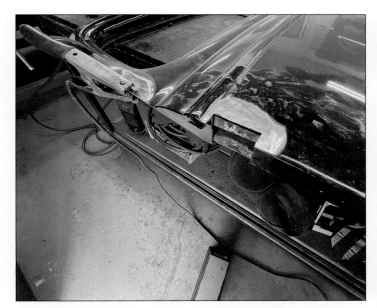

On the bench, Connole removed the middle hinge from the passenger door and is preparing to move it up to the center of the beltline.

Using suitable 16-gauge sheet metal, Connole made a small filler piece to fill the hole in the door where the middle hinge once was.

Once completed, Connole TIG welded the filler piece into the door. Some builders might not bother to move the hinge, but it looks more balanced and provides better support after it was moved.

On the passenger's side, the middle hinge was moved up to the center of the beltline. In addition, Connole made a filler for where the original hinge was, which was used as part of the support structure.

On the driver's side, the original hinge position on the door was filled, and the hinge was moved up.

A 1933 coupe door is pretty heavy, so Brian Sloma helped lift it into position. I was surprised at how well the door fit the first time.

Connole uses his secret weapon: the Hinge-O-Liner from Thomas Kearney's Leading Edge Machine & Design. Its adjustable design allows you to achieve precise hinge alignment.

You can see where the middle hinge was relocated to the center of the beltline. This spreads the load when only two hinges are used.

Connole previously sanded away the paint from the area where he intended to make his cut. In addition, he applied some Dykem and marked his cut line.

The driver's side of the top was similarly sanded and marked out. Note that the middle hinge was already moved upward.

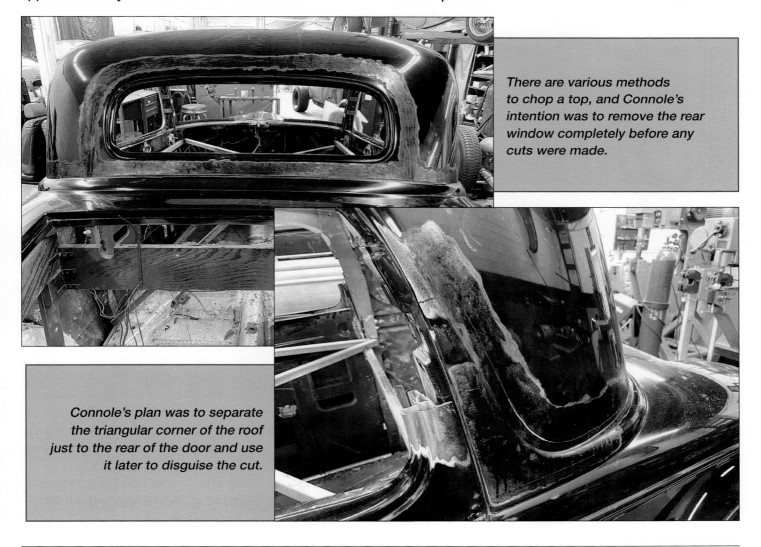

There are various methods to chop a top, and Connole's intention was to remove the rear window completely before any cuts were made.

Connole's plan was to separate the triangular corner of the roof just to the rear of the door and use it later to disguise the cut.

After marking his proposed cut lines, Connole asked Sloma to hold the door while he made his first cut with the reciprocating saw.

After slicing through the A-post of the door, Connole moved to the B-post and sliced through that as well. If you don't have help, you could always work on a bench.

Sloma holds the top of the door, which was removed. The A-post is where the second cut will be made, eliminating the top hinge.

While Sloma secures the front of the door, Connole cuts the B-post with the reciprocating saw. At this time, he is not cutting more out of the doorframe.

Using the reciprocating saw, Connole makes a second cut on the door's A-post. You could also use a cut-off wheel for this part of the process.

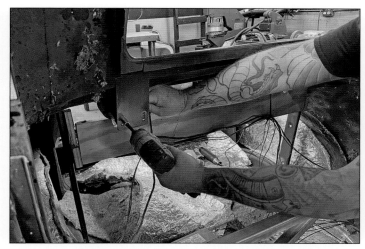

Before cutting the roof, Connole removed the brackets that secure the wooden window mechanism support from the roof structure.

Using an air-powered cut-off wheel, Connole began removing the rear window in one piece. This is not the method that everyone uses, but it works for Connole.

The cut-off wheel is not always the right tool for the job. Here, Connole switched to a Snap-on air-powered reciprocating saw for the cut directly below the window.

The reciprocating saw was more suitable for cutting around the curve of the rear window.

The rear window frame is removed from the roof and put aside until the height of the final chop is determined.

Connole moved onward to the corner of the roof. Here, he uses the Snap-on reciprocating air saw to separate the top from the body.

Cannole performs the vertical cut with a cut-off wheel. As you gain experience, you'll get the feel for the tool that is best suited for the job.

Henry Ford advertised that there was no wood in his cars. However, there was oak behind the door to support the hinges as well as an upper door header. This was a modern replacement kit.

Connole cuts into the front A-posts with a reciprocating saw. Small imperfections in height can be easily repaired.

After Connole had severed both front posts and rear posts, the top was lifted clear of the body.

It's scary to see the roof on the floor of the shop next to the car. You may wonder if the two will ever be one again. Now, the real work begins.

Using a reciprocating saw, Connole cut the A-pillars, removing a 4½-inch section. Model 40 posts are much more tapered than Deuce posts.

The door supports were not original on this car. Even though they were oak, they were not difficult to cut. Note the support structure inside the car.

The roof was put back on the car to see how it looks and aligns. Notice that the 4½-inch chop puts the top of the A-pillars behind the bottom of the A-pillars.

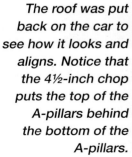

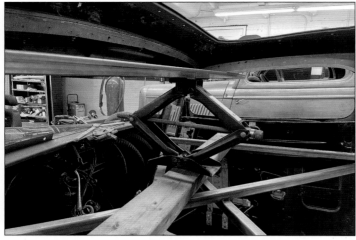

To support the front end of the roof while he was reviewing it, Connole used a regular scissor jack that is supported by a 2x4 piece of lumber on the support structure.

This corner piece was removed when the roof was cut away. It was to be used later and was massaged to fit.

The inner wood frame that provides support for the doorjamb and hinges will be massaged later, depending on the final cut of the roof.

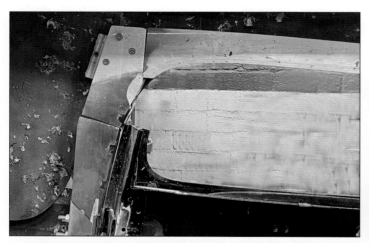

The inner structure of the A-pillars is not as complicated as the 1932 coupe A-pillar, but the taper is greater.

While this chop was only in the mock-up stage, Connole made some small steel plates to hold the wood in position.

He then moved back to the front and began cutting into the back of the A-pillars with an angle grinder that had a large-diameter cut-off wheel.

Because of the convoluted inner structure, Connole had to use several cutting tools to get through it all. Here, he's using the reciprocating saw.

Having chopped more than a few cars, Connole made the decision to remove the lower section of the windshield. Here, the cut line across the cowl is marked with a black permanent marker.

Connole switched back to the air-powered reciprocating saw to make the cut across the cowl. Years of doing this have given him a good eye for such work.

Connole removes the complete lower section of the windshield after slicing through the inner structure of the A-pillars and sawing across the cowl.

The point where everything is separated and nothing is joined together is a scary moment if you've never chopped a top before. Don't be discouraged; it will come together.

The driver-side A-pillar's inner structure shows what Connole had to cut through. Although it's somewhat complicated, it's nothing that welding can't fix.

With the roof flipped upside down on the bench, Connole offered up the lower part of the windshield to see how much finagling that he has to do.

After removing 4½ inches from the A-pillars, they no longer align. So, work is necessary to make them right.

Experience dictated that Connole cut into the back of the base of the A-pillar where it joins the cowl so that he could spread the pillars apart.

Connole moved onward to the roof. Using a permanent marker, he drew some cut lines onto the backside of the header panel.

After cutting four slots into the roof header panel (two at the front and one at each side), Connole and Sloma lift the roof back into position.

Using the large-diameter cut-off wheel on an angle grinder, Connole cuts slots into the header panel.

O'Connell, the car's owner, stopped in to see the progress that was being made. It's not always a good idea to let the customer see his car hacked to pieces, but O'Connell loved it.

The roof was removed once again, as Connole needed to work on the A-pillars. In addition, it's interesting to compare O'Connell's car with Houck's.

Connole cuts the rear of the A-pillar with a reciprocating saw.

This close-up of the bottom of the A-pillar shows the angled cut that Connole made, which continues the angle of the windshield.

As Connole pushes the driver-side A-pillar forward to see how it will eventually line up, the slots that were cut into the roof on the passenger's side are visible.

The A-pillar on the passenger's side shows where the corner cuts were made. The bottom of the windshield will eventually be pushed out to meet the cowl.

From the driver's side, its clear how much the realignment of the A-pillar opens up the cowl by more than 1 inch.

The A-pillar on Darren's coupe provides a great reference for the way that the pillars were shaped after the chop and how the eyebrow tapers into the pillar.

On the passenger's side, the misalignment of top and bottom is evident after the 4½ inches were removed.

Connole took some measurements just to make sure that he was on track for a final windshield height of 7 inches in the middle.

Finagling was necessary to align all of the sectioned pieces of the A-pillar. You just have to make it all fit.

Connole's next task was to hammer out a bowl shape that was eventually going to go into the front corner of the roof.

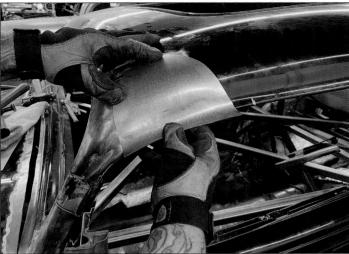

Connole is offering up the bowl-shaped insert that will eventually give his A-pillar-to-roof joint and nice flow.

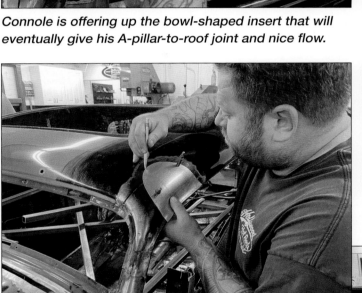

Connole uses a few Clecos to position his patch so that he can mark out the area in the roof to be removed.

Blue Dykem, which is $15 to $20 per can, was used to coat the area to be cut.

After he carefully marked where his patch would go, Connole uses an air-powered cut-off wheel to begin his cut.

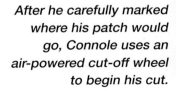

After making the initial cut with the cut-off wheel, Connole uses an air-powered saw to complete the cut.

Having achieved a nice, clean cut for the insert, Connole cleaned off the Dykem using carburetor cleaner or lacquer thinner.

Because it was difficult to clamp, Connole hand held the insert in place while he tacked it into position.

Connole added a few more tacks to hold the insert. Some massaging at the top will be necessary.

There will be some mis-alignment until everything is pushed into place. Connole uses a skin spoon to lift the roof into position.

Connole uses a combination of lifting and tapping to get all of the pieces properly aligned before hammering the welds.

With his left hand, Connole uses another body spoon to support the underside while he hammers on the top side.

After the insert on the driver's side was tacked into position, Connole lifted up the door top just to see how it looked.

It's not easy to duplicate something that looks simple but has compound curves. Nevertheless, an insert also had to be formed for the passenger's side.

The A-pillars of many early Ford cars appear to have been beaten and leaded at the top of the post where they meet the roof.

To eliminate the ugliness, Connole fabricated a new outer skin as a replacement for the original factory part.

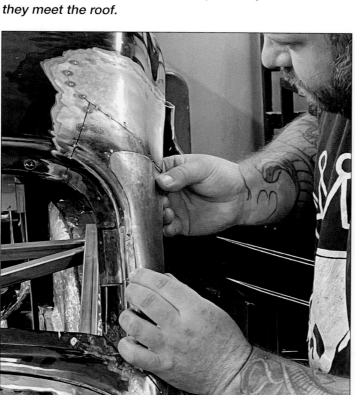

Let's call this part on the A-pillar "the spoon." Here, Connole lays the spoon over the A-pillar and is ready to mark the metal to be removed.

After marking the area to be removed, Connole uses a cut-off wheel to remove the unwanted material.

HOW TO CHOP TOPS

With the top of the A-pillar removed, the inner structure can be seen as well as the square tube that is used to brace the windshield.

Once again, judicious grinding and hammering was required to make the spoon fit the hole in the A-pillar.

After the spoon was carefully positioned into the A-pillar and clamped into place, Connole tacked it into position.

The spoon was stitched into the A-pillar. However, there is still plenty of shaping to do.

On the passenger's side, you can expect that the corresponding pillar was equally beaten and filled. This time, it was filled with brass rather than lead—scary.

After performing work on the passenger's side that was similar to the driver's side, Connole is getting the top into shape. Note the bottom of the pillar.

After getting the outside of the A-pillars into shape, Connole moved on to the underside, where he began shaping strips of metal to fill the inner frame.

Connole cut various parts and pieces for the inner structure.

Connole clamps the various components of the inner structure together while Sloma gives us a thumbs up.

More than clamps and one pair of hands were required at this point. Connole holds the parts in position while Sloma handles the welding.

After all of the work to get the passenger-side A-pillar to this stage, the finished product looks as factory as possible.

From the back, you can see that the top of the roof was lowered into the body and Cleco'd into position.

The roof was dropped down inside the body before the roof was cut.

Connole holds up the corner of the reveal to see how it is going to slot into the lowered top.

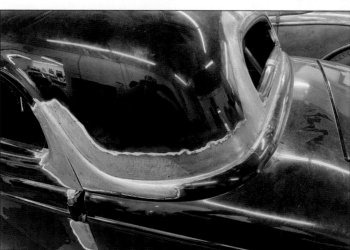

The driver's side and rear window were contoured and finish welded.

The reveal corner was welded in and smoothed out. You can see where the rear of the door window was pie cut.

Even after the chop, the rear window remains a good size to provide a reasonable view out of the rear.

Once the door window frames were finalized, it was time to begin work on the hard-to-find garnish moldings.

On its own, the driver's door window frame has a slightly odd shape, but this will go unnoticed after it has been installed.

The rear corner of the passenger-side garnish molding was welded up. Notice the small fillet in the corner that matches the outer frame.

Where there is a lack of paint, some work was done. In this case, the hinge was moved up.

This is the completed inner window garnish molding. The parts were marked so that they wouldn't get mixed up.

This view of the corresponding door-jamb striker shows where the hinge was moved up and the resultant gap was filled.

Desiring a race-car theme, O'Connell requested a louvered roof insert, and Marcio Luz began by fabricating an aluminum surround.

After making the frame, Luz wheeled up an aluminum panel that O'Connell will be able to open from inside the car.

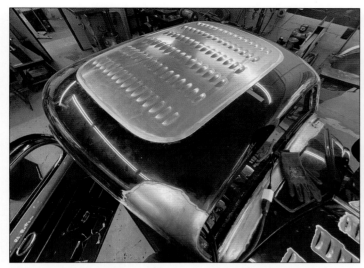

The louvered roof panel is in position. Notice how the soft-edged louvers align with those in the hood. All of the louvers were punched in-house at Hollywood Hot Rods.

This is how the louvered roof insert looks from inside the car. At this point, the hinge mechanism had not yet been fabricated.

The rear decklid is ready to receive the louver treatment with six rows of staggered louvers.

Desiring the early 1960s drag race, hot rod look, Don had Hollywood Hot Rods punch six rows of louvers into the original steel hood.

While the roof was removed, this simple, single-hoop roll bar was installed. It is bolted through the floor to the frame rails.

These are two dissimilar coupes. Houck's 1934 coupe is in bare metal with a LaSalle grille in the background. In the foreground is O'Connell's 1933 coupe, which will eventually be painted white.

Despite all of the cutting, the windshield actually looks factory—even where the cowl was filled.

The three friends who performed the top chop on O'Connell's 1933 3-window coupe are (from left to right) Geoff Wheeless, Connole, and Luz.

ROLLING BONES: SCHMIDT & SUCKLING 1934 COUPE

Text by Jon Suckling, Photos by Ken Schmidt and Jon Suckling

Ken Schmidt and Keith Cornell founded the Rolling Bones Hot Rod Shop several decades ago, working out of an old cow barn in Upstate New York. They built early Fords in the dry lakes/Bonneville style, right out of the pages of a Don Montgomery book. Their signature style has become its own look, but there was a time several decades ago when a heavy lakes chop, cowl steering, patina, and numbers on doors were rare. Those old race cars had faded away like an old photo, but Schmidt and Cornell helped to bring them back.

During the 10 years that it took to build the Rolling Bones Schmidt & Suckling (S&S) coupe, we often joked that the 1934 Ford would be Schmidt's swan song, but we never thought it would become a reality. Sadly, Schmidt passed away in March 2023. He put his heart and soul into the S&S coupe. It was to be the ultimate Rolling Bones creation with no compromises—from the 392 Hemi engine to the 10-inch chop, and it was built to run on the Bonneville salt.

Schmidt was an accomplished fine artist, painting scenes of the old West, so he had an eye for balance and proportion that was unlike other car builders. We spent years talking about this car and planning the details, and it took thousands of hours to turn that vision into cold steel.

The Pierson Brothers and SO-CAL 1934 coupes were inspirations for the S&S coupe. Adding to the competition-coupe formula of a heavy chop and track nose were a multitude of other details to simplify the lines of the car. These details, including the tucked tail (altering the usual ducktail rear profile to follow the circumference of the rear tire) may go unnoticed to the untrained eye.

Another subtle but time-consuming change was the addition of 1932 hood sides and the deletion of the Model 40 fender well "bubbles." This involved lowering the cowl and fabricating new frame rails forward of the firewall. Removing the center door hinge was also important to the styling—many take the easy path

and simply delete the roof hinge, but as Ken always said, "The center hinge catches the eye and slows the car down visually."

The most dramatic statement is the drastic 10-inch chop. Although the coupe was built to run at Bonneville, it was not built to comply with Southern California Timing Association (SCTA) rules, which meant that, unlike the Pierson and SO-CAL coupes, we were not restricted by a minimum windshield height. This allowed Schmidt to use a cut-down screen frame, retain the opening mechanism, and give the car a much better appearance.

Even with such a severe chop, Schmidt ensured that the cut looked as "factory" as possible, retaining the various swage lines and moldings, so that it looks like it might have escaped from Edsel's Special Vehicles Department. Schmidt's artist background dictated that the proportions were crucial. The windshield was laid back about 40 degrees and given a slight wedge, thereby keeping the roof turret length in proportion to the body by eliminating the need to add an awkward filler piece to the screen post.

The cuts at the rear of the roof were relatively easy. The real skill was at the front, where it was a 3-D jigsaw puzzle to work out where that S-shaped cut above the front pillar had to go—not to mention to ensure that the chop matched perfectly on both sides.

Physically cutting the car was fairly straight forward, but great care was taken to measure, mark, and tape the cuts, which was followed by countless hours refining and leading the roof and doors. As this was effectively Schmidt's own car, he completed every part of the car to his own high standard, irrespective of how long it took.

Just before he died, Ken Schmidt wrote about the art of chopping tops.

"More than any other body modification, the chop defines the attitude and creates the look of a hot rod," he wrote. "Imagine the midnight oil that was burnt the week after the first coupe with a deep chop showed up at the salt flats.

"With a chop of about 10 inches, the Schmidt & Suckling 1934 3-window coupe was built not only to pay homage to those postwar lakes cars but also to kick up the dust of El Mirage and the East Coast Timing Association (ECTA) mile speed events, to burn rubber at the nostalgia drags, to terrorize the highways, and to taste the salt of Bonneville at the World of Speed.

"For a successful chop, the lines and proportions of the entire body must work together. We make our sail-panel cut about an inch above the reveal (rather than straight across the center) for two reasons: 1) being close to the reveal reduces the chance of warping and 2) it's easy to simply make vertical cuts down to the reveal to lean the bottom of the roof slightly forward."

The Schmidt & Suckling (S&S) coupe sits at the Rolling Bones barn in Greenfield Center, New York. The area to be cut was scuffed clean of primer and marked with tape. Cutting an inch above the reveal helps to prevent warping.

Owners are invited to help build their hot rods at Rolling Bones. Jon Suckling's wife, Jacqueline Suckling, uses a jigsaw to cut the roof.

Jacqueline, Jon, and Keith Cornell lift the severed roof from the body.

"After slipping the roof down inside the body, we step back," said Ken Schmidt of Rolling Bones. "Usually, the owners will just stare in disbelief. We call it 'instant attitude.'"

After being cut out of the roof, the bottom of the rear window was dropped down to the reveal and tacked back onto the body.

This shows how the rear mail-slot window will look after the top is lowered into the body.

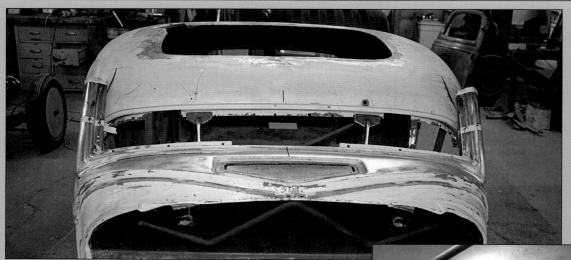

With such a radical chop, the top falls far into the body. Schmidt's plan was for a radical 10-inch chop.

The rear passenger-side corner of the roof opening is in need of repair.

Stripped of paint, the roof was cut about 1 inch above the reveal to help prevent warping. Some fit and fudging is necessary.

The fadeaway of the drip rail was marked with a permanent marker. This line and proportion provides the attitude. Eliminate lines that go backward.

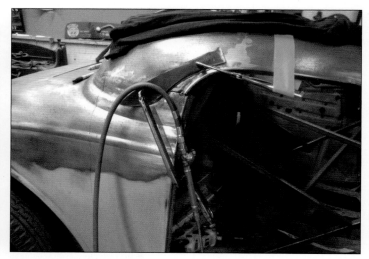

Rolling Bones formed a dolly that was clamped into position. Using a torch and hammers, the swoopy reveal was beaten into shape.

The reveal at the end of the drip rail was beaten into shape. Everything leans forward to accentuate the profile.

The seam around the back of the roof was welded and hammer welded for a smooth finish, and the drip rail now flows into the body.

The A-pillar was tacked to the roof and the shape of the "spoon" was defined with a permanent marker.

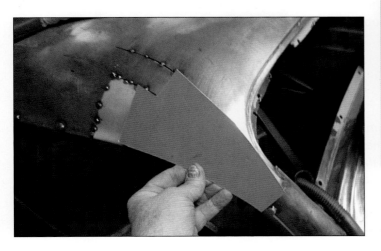

This cardboard template was used to form the spoon that fits the front corner of the roof.

Using the previously shown template, the front corner of the roof was removed. Note the use of a steel strap to tie the roof to the A-pillar.

The spoon was let into the roof and tacked into position. In addition, notice the split going up into the roof.

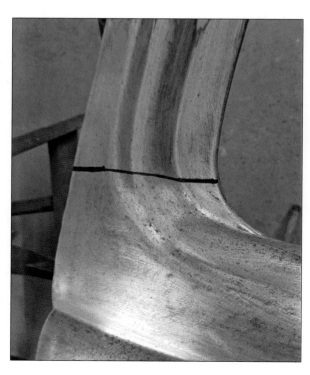

Moving onward to the doors, a permanent marker was used to indicate where the doors will be cut. Note the fillet in the back of a 1934 coupe door.

A similar cut line was marked at the front of the door just above the hole for the door lock. However, another deeper cut has to be made.

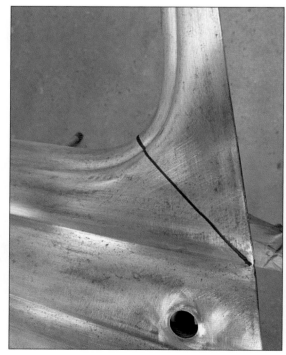

After the front of the door was cut, a deeper (or more laid back) cut was necessary for this extreme chop.

The door and the severed window frame are on a lightweight tubular workstand. Note that the middle hinge will be eliminated.

With the door clamped and held into position with lengths of angle iron tacked in place, it is clear that the middle hinge must be removed.

Jon Suckling (left) and Cornell hold the severed doorframe to show what the removal of 10 inches looks like.

Cornell (left) and Schmidt offer up the sectioned door top on the driver's side. Notice the difference in curvatures between the door and the roof.

The gap in the doorframe was filled using a piece of frame that was salvaged from the previously removed sections.

Cut to the extreme, the rear of the door top was tacked and taped into position. There's a significant gap at the back where the curvatures are different. With parts of the doorframe tacked into position, it's obvious that the window frame needs an insert and that some extra metal needs to be added.

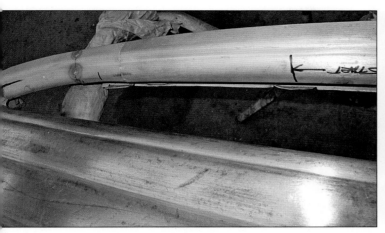

The section of extra doorframe was tacked into position. This is like a jigsaw, where you make your own pieces.

Tacked into position, the window frame fills the hole but needs some additional metal for perfect fitment.

Schmidt placed masking tape around the edge of the doorframe to see where additional material needs to be added.

Measurements were taken and marked on the lip of the doorframe to indicate where metal needed to be added to fill the gap.

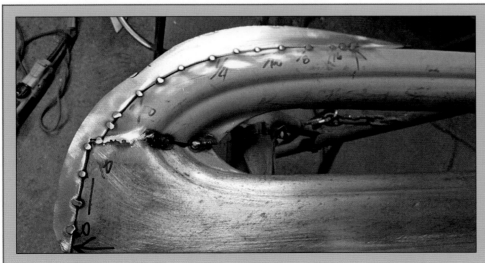

A sliver of steel was added to the door edge. Next, it will be shaved down to even out the door gaps.

The door is coming together, and some steel bar stock was tacked around the top edge of the doorframe.

Schmidt did not like the middle hinge. It was removed, and the top hinge was moved down.

Using the correct welding rod, the shortened hinges were tacked together before being trial-fit.

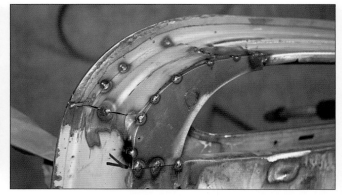

The doors required some patching on the inside to fill the various gaps that were made by the sectioning.

Using a permanent marker, the hinge was marked where it will be cut. Be sure to check the hinge material before you begin this cut.

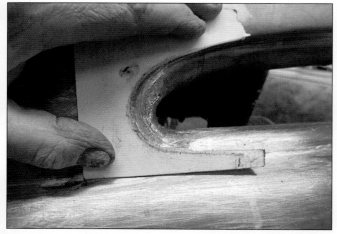

A cardboard template was used for the rear window and the side windows.

Welded, ground, and leaded, the leading edge of the side window is well shaped at this point. In addition, the door gap looks good.

The top looks quite natural. Notice that the fillet was retained at the rear of the window.

Some cuts were made to lower the cowl, and a knife blade of steel was added between the cowl and the base of the windshield.

Here with a coating of lead, the cowl, which had to be lowered to get that Bonneville profile, is taking shape.

A significant gap opened up after the cowl was cut in front of the windshield to be able to lean the posts back at 40 degrees.

These are just a few of the dollies that were used to knock this beast into shape. According to Schmidt, the roof was previously filled and finished with braze, lead, and body filler.

After a great deal of shaping, the front of the roof and the windshield have come together. Note the holes in the header for the windshield hinges.

With a 10-inch chop, that windshield is small, and it's laid back at 40 degrees. Nevertheless, Schmidt made it work even with the original hinges.

The inner doorframe, header panel, and more were fabricated from Swiss cheese steel for a race-car look.

Before the hood louvers and before the paint, the S&S coupe appeared at the Grand National Roadster Show in 2018.

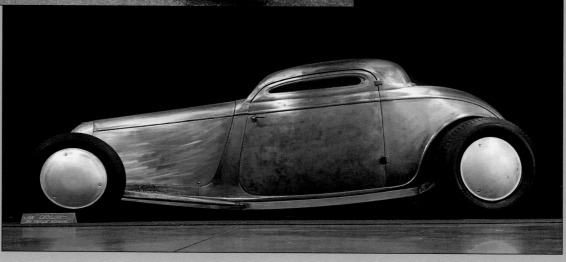

The S&S coupe has a radical profile, but because of the curvature of the frame and the beauty of the chop, the car does not look broken.

The track roadster–style grille was formed by Cornell and Schmidt, and some bars were fabricated by Jon Suckling.

With flat wheel discs, an opening windshield, and a whole lot of louvers, the S&S coupe is one of the most dramatic hot rods that has been built in the modern era. (Photo Courtesy Jim Leggett)

The S&S coupe is at home on the Bonneville Salt Flats, where Schmidt envisioned it. (Photo Courtesy Jim Leggett)

ROY BRIZIO STREET RODS: JEFF BECK'S 1934 FORD 5-WINDOW COUPE

I've known guitarist Jeff Beck since I was a teenager—not because of his music but because of his love for hot rods. We met in the United Kingdom (UK) in what Brits call a paper shop (a newsstand in the US). We were both looking at hot rod magazines and struck up a conversation. It turned out that we didn't live far from each other, so we began hanging out and talking about cars.

As I got to know Beck, I realized that he liked to do a lot of his own work—from sand blasting frame rails to wiring. We spent many hours in a cold, damp British garage (that was actually an old scout hut), taking bits off one car to get another one running. It was an endless task because the damp atmosphere rusted everything, but we had lots of fun, and I learned a lot. In fact, Beck was instrumental (pun intended) in helping me build my first Deuce roadster.

Even after I immigrated to the US, we stayed in touch and went to some hot rod events together, and I'd go to watch him play.

Over the years, Beck worked with numerous American hot rod builders to supply chassis and parts, including Pete and Jake's Hot Rod Parts. However, Beck eventually settled with Roy Brizio Street Rods in South San Francisco, California, and Brizio has built or helped Beck build numerous rods. I don't know how many hot rods Beck owned (10 or maybe 12). Brizio built some of them, and he partially built others and then shipped them to Beck, who finished them at home. If Brizio put a new chassis under a car, then Beck liked to take the old frame and build something else. He didn't mind "getting stuck in" and was quite crafty in his own way.

A few years ago, Beck contacted Bobby Walden of Walden Speed Shop in Pomona, California, about a tribute to the famed Mooneyham & Sharp 1934 5-window coupe. Walden built one of his signature frames for Beck and installed a blown Buick Nailhead. As cool as they are, Beck didn't want a Nailhead. Eventually, the car went to Brizio, who replaced the Buick engine with a small-block Chevy and replaced the Oldsmobile rear end with a 9-inch Ford. They were not particularly interesting choices, but, as I previously wrote, Beck enjoyed working on his cars and swapping things around. Nearly all of his cars had a small-block Chevy engine and a 9-inch rear end. He knew how to rebuild a 9-inch rear end.

There was nothing wrong with Walden's work. In fact, the roof chop was superbly executed, and the way that Walden metal-finished it remains how it is today. Sadly, Beck died unexpectedly in 2023.

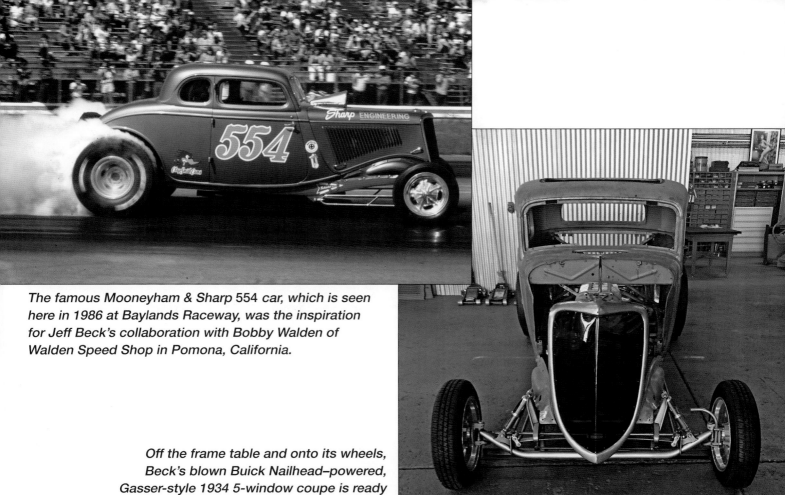

The famous Mooneyham & Sharp 554 car, which is seen here in 1986 at Baylands Raceway, was the inspiration for Jeff Beck's collaboration with Bobby Walden of Walden Speed Shop in Pomona, California.

Off the frame table and onto its wheels, Beck's blown Buick Nailhead–powered, Gasser-style 1934 5-window coupe is ready for a top chop.

Stance is important, and this one sits about right, especially with the long hairpin radius rods and spindle Halibrand wheels. It needs some height off the top, though.

The inner support structure that holds the body together features Walden's use of turn buckles.

Walden begins by chopping the doors. Before doing so, he makes wooden templates to make sure that both sides end up exactly the same.

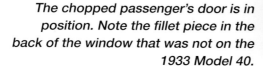

The chopped passenger's door is in position. Note the fillet piece in the back of the window that was not on the 1933 Model 40.

Most of the Model 40s that I have photographed have had this area of the A-pillar beaten down and filled with lead at the factory.

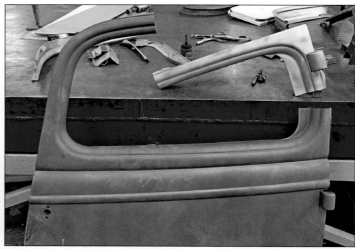

Walden removed the rear corner of the door. He will retain the top hinge because Model 40 suicide doors are heavy.

The top hinge was retained but is now located farther down (in the middle of the rear side window).

Both doors were hung before Walden began the roof chop. The blown Buick engine was later replaced.

Walden began by removing the upper portion of the A-pillars. Note the strap that is holding the A-pillars together as well as the markings on the door top.

The upper part of the A-pillar shows where Walden is making his cuts. The Model 40 has no rain gutter; it only has an eyebrow.

Before Walden cut the roof, he shaped up these pieces that would eventually form the corners of the rear side windows.

After marking with Dykem, the rear corner of the roof was carefully removed. A new piece will be shaped to fit the lower profile.

The panel that has been shaped for the rear corner of the roof is visible as well as the panel that was shaped for the lower rear corner of the side window.

This photo shows how the jigsaw puzzle of panels fits together to form the rear quarter of the roof.

The header panel was tack welded into position, and you can also see the beginning of the shaping at the top of the A-pillar.

This view of the windshield opening shows that the cowl vent was retained. The workmanship is meticulous.

In true Gasser fashion and as a tribute to the original Mooneyham & Sharp 554 car, Beck's coupe had a red Lexan roof insert.

The jigsaw puzzle is coming together, as the rear panel was tack welded into position. In addition, the lower corner of the side window is now complete.

After the panel was tack welded into position, the seam was hammer welded before it was ground smooth.

This top has been hammer welded and sanded to a finish worthy of Henry Ford's approval. You'd never be able to tell that the top had been cut.

As the rear came together so did the A-pillars. Notice how smoothly the eyebrow rolls neatly down into the A-pillar.

Out in the California sun after a huge amount of fabrication work, Beck's tribute to the 554 coupe has an identity of its own.

1936 FORD 3-WINDOW COUPES

Ever since Herb Reneau chopped Jack Calori's 1936 3-window coupe that became the first chopped car to appear on the cover of *Hot Rod* magazine in November 1949, the 1935 Model 48 (and the 1936 Model 68 to a much greater extent) has been on the chopping board.

The reasons are multifaceted. First, with only 2 inches removed, the 1935–1936 coupes take on a completely different look—an appearance that looks like it should have come from the factory that way. The lowered profile accentuates the sleekness of an already-sleek design. The green-

house of a 1935 model and the 1936 model is extremely tapered, making the chop one of the most difficult of the early Fords to execute, but when it is done well, it transforms the car.

Unfortunately, no one was chopping a 1936 model as this book was coming together. However, I was lucky to find photographs of three different chops. They took place at SO-CAL Speed Shop and at the Kennedy Brothers Bomb Factory, which are both in Pomona, California. So, I pieced together each shop's approach to provide a look at the process.

The first car was chopped at

SO-CAL by master metal shaper Bill "Birdman" Stewart. Stewart was meticulous in his work, and maybe it took longer than it should have, but his work and attention to detail regarding door gaps and alignment was exemplary. Sadly, I lost track of the name of the owner, but Stewart did an excellent job.

The second car was James Jard's 1936 coupe, which was chopped by Jay Kennedy at the Kennedy Brothers Bomb Factory in Pomona, California. Jay also chopped the final example that belonged to Mike Ness of the band Social Distortion.

Bill "Birdman" Stewart's 1936 Ford 3-Window Coupe

Bill "Birdman" Stewart is working on the window frames of a 1936 3-window coupe at Pete Chapouris's SO-CAL Speed Shop in Pomona, California. The top has already been lowered and tacked into position.

Stewart Cleco'd steel plates across the door gaps to keep them aligned with the body because there were no locks or hinges on the body.

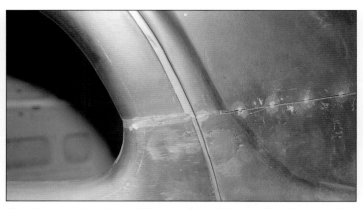

Besides the tacking of the roof and the welded joint in the corner of the door, this image shows the strip of metal that Stewart used to maintain consistent door gaps.

This is the gap in the window frame that occurs when the roof is stretched. If you're lucky, you'll have some spare material. If you're not lucky, you'll need to fabricate a filler piece.

This is the underside of the side of the roof where Stewart stretched it. Stretching the roof is necessary when the A-pillars aren't raked.

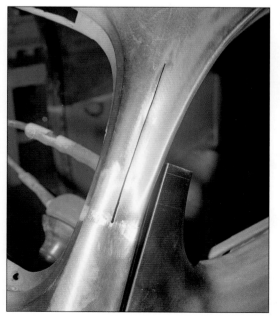

The driver-side A-pillar shows where Stewart made a vertical cut up the post to reduce its width and align it with the bottom of the post.

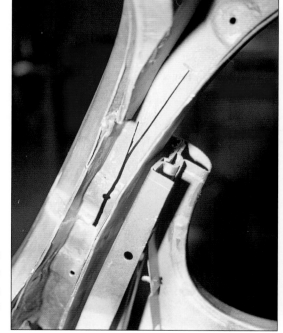

On the passenger's side, Stewart made similar slots on the inner structure to facilitate alignment.

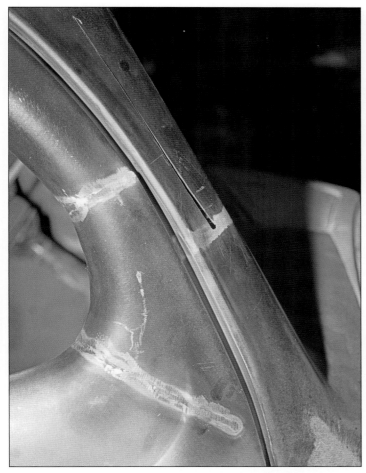

The A-pillar shows where Stewart made his pie cut in the corner and where the upper cut was made in the window frame. In addition, note the slot in the A-pillar.

As Stewart works to fill the gap in the window frame, he uses bits of scrap to align the two halves.

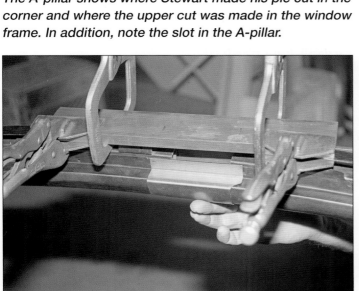

With the two halves of the window frame clamped into position, Stewart folded some sheet metal that he will trim to fill the gap.

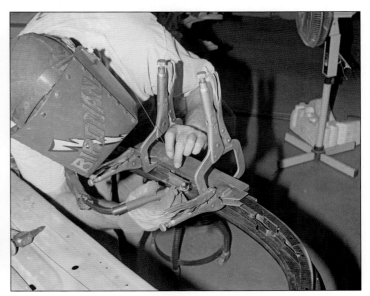

Having folded his filler piece from scrap sheet metal, Stewart TIG welded the fillet into position.

James Jard's 1936 Ford 3-Window Coupe

James Jard's 1936 Ford 3-window coupe awaits a top chop at the Kennedy Brothers Bomb Factory in Pomona, California. Note that Jay already repaired the bottom of the body.

This shows how tapered the top of a 1936 Ford Model 68 is when compared to earlier Fords. Note the welded tab to hold the door closed, as there are no latches.

With the passenger door removed, the extensive support framework is visible. As with most of these structures, it's made from 1-inch square tubing.

In this case, Jay will stretch the roof rather than rake the posts to make the A-pillars align.

Jay used some steel plates clamped into position to hold the front of the roof in position while he tack welded the rear.

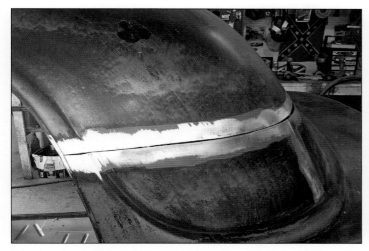

The back of the roof was sectioned and cleaned up to align with the bottom. Note the vertical split that is necessary to shrink the bottom.

On the driver's side, Jay has the door installed so that he can begin shaping the window frames. You can see the area where the top has been extended.

Although it has been disguised with black primer, you can still see where Jay sectioned the roof and the area where he cut a vertical slit to pull the body inward.

After Jay completed all of the bodywork, Jard's 1936 Ford 3-window coupe moved over to his brother Joe, who handles all of the paint at the Kennedy Brothers Bomb Factory.

As with a lot of smart guys in the hot rod business, Joe uses colors that are not overly complicated—those that can be painted as they are without too much worry about color matching.

With only 2 inches of height removed, it's difficult to tell if a 1936 Ford has been chopped or not. However, a chopped top certainly looks better than a stock top.

The ocean-deep color of Jard's coupe is a special Kennedy Brothers mix that's similar to a factory 1951 Mercury color.

Jard's Oldsmobile-powered 1936 coupe is a mild custom hot rod fitted with a 1941 Ford front bumper. It has been lowered and has black running boards and minimal chrome.

Mike Ness's 1936 Ford 3-Window Coupe

When I caught up with the chop of Mike Ness's 1936 3-window coupe, Jay Kennedy was just starting. This side of the rear roof has been nicely finished, but the A-pillar has yet to be moved.

Looking through the car into the driver's side, you can see the cross where the roof was split horizontally and vertically. That side has yet to be finish welded.

This shows that the rear quarter was finished, but the front of the roof where the factory weld is located has yet to be moved forward.

A slice has been taken out of the roof to move the top of the A-pillar forward. Note the round bar that has been welded between the two roof sections to hold them in line.

On the driver's side, Jay is using a ratchet strap to hold the front pillars together. The front pillars are aligned, and the roof is split.

Jay sliced up the roof and then pulled the front section forward until the A-pillars aligned.

Jay cut and folded some sheet metal to fill the gap in the roof. At the moment, this was only tacked into position.

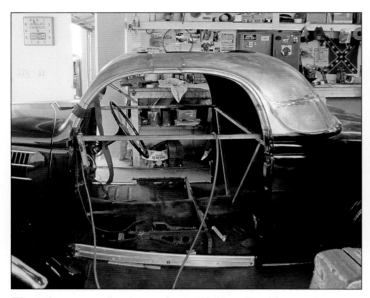

That door opening has a beautiful profile. You can see the flowing shape of the reveal around the door and where Jay began hammer welding around the roof.

With some primer on the top, Jay moved his attention to the window frames, which, of course, need to be stretched in the middle, possibly with some leftover material.

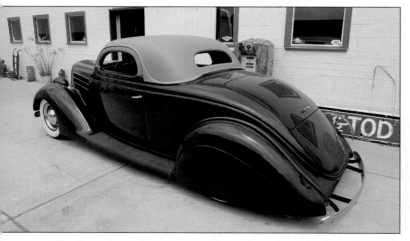

The long tapering rear end is a signature design piece of the 1935 and 1936 Fords. It looks good, especially when it is enhanced with fender skirts and a chopped top.

Jay connected the A-pillar. Note that the 1936 3-window coupe, as with the Model 40, also has no gutter to deal with.

In the middle of the window frame, Jay added some material to stretch the frame.

Ever since Herb Reneau chopped Jack Calori's 1936 coupe in the late 1940s, builders have been chasing the dream of simple perfection. Mike Ness's car comes close.

CORNFIELD CUSTOMS: 1940 CADILLAC LASALLE MODEL 50

Who chops a 1940 Cadillac LaSalle coupe? Mike Wagner of Cornfield Customs—that's who. As a land speed racer, I knew about Cornfield Customs because I saw the company's *Rouster Spl.* aluminum-bodied Indy-style roadster at Bonneville in 2020. I love Indy roadsters, and to see one driving on the street and the salt was astonishing. The aluminum workmanship of Mike Wagner of Cornfield Customs was exceptional.

"[Wagner] got into automotive metal shaping because he wanted to build himself a Model A," according to Baileigh Industrial, a company with whom Wagner works. "His talent and promise quickly impressed a seasoned hot rod fabricator."

"I knew nothing about hot rods," Wagner said. "I went to vocational school for welding and machining. I knew how to do basic machining processes, and I met this old guy who'd been building hot rods since the 1950s. He was like, 'Man, you're pretty good at this. You should quit your job.'

"And that's exactly what I did. So, at 20 years old, I quit my production TIG welding job and just opened up a shop."

Wagner is known for the quality of his work.

"Some people will tell you that I'm known for metal shaping, some people will say [that I'm known for] tube chassis, and other guys will say [that I'm known for] traditional hot rod chassis," Wagner said. "In the beginning, it was traditional hot rod stuff. I kind of evolved into making door skins and quarter panels for those, which then led to more exotic stuff, such as aluminum-bodied race cars and exotic European stuff."

The car that grabbed my attention was a rear roof section of a customer's 1940 Cadillac LaSalle (the last year for production for that model). Wagner's process is interesting and inspiring. In addition, check out the various social media sites for Cornfield Customs and its advanced metal-shaping class.

Mike Wagner's hand-formed Indy-style roadster Rouster Spl. *is shown on the salt at Bonneville in 2020. The body is completely hand-formed aluminum, which sits on one of Mike Wagner's chassis.*

The original concept for the LaSalle was drawn by Chris Piscitelli from Detroit, where he earned a degree in design at the College for Creative Studies.

The serious work is about to begin, and Wagner stripped the paint that was on the roof. Note the split windshield and the forward rake of the B-pillars.

The factory roof seams were filled with lead that should be removed—unless you prefer lead over filler.

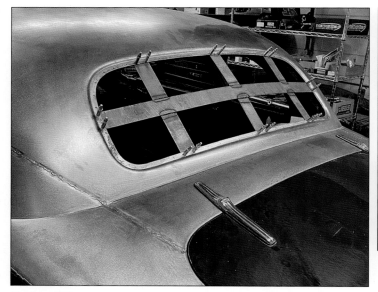

Before Wagner cut into the roof, he used heavy pieces of 2-inch steel strapping that was Cleco'd into position to hold the rear window frame together.

Wagner already lowered the top and is tacking the B-pillar. He made Lexan templates for the rear side windows.

The A-pillars have been laid back and the doors are in the process of being chopped. The chop makes that grille even more dramatic.

With the rear window being laid down, you can see what aligns and what doesn't align.

The old roof has been cut, and the doors and rear side windows are partway done.

This close-up shows the new panel that Wagner is making to go between the roof and the gutter. In addition, it shows how the top of the doorframe is being extended.

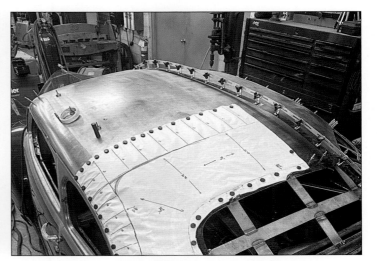

Unlike most choppers, Wagner uses white masking paper to form his templates. The paper is held in position with small magnets.

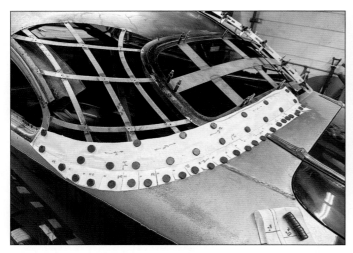

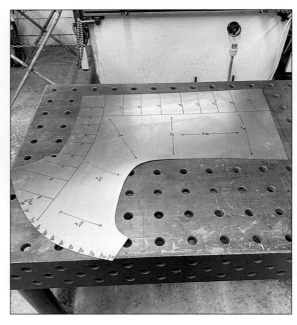

The paper template for the rear roof quarter has been transferred to sheet metal. Note the precise measurements.

After making a template for the rear roof quarter, Wagner used more paper to make the template for the roof-to-decklid transition.

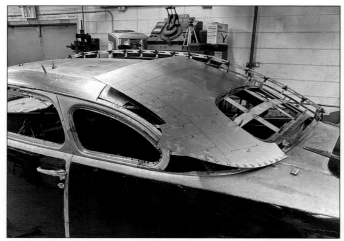

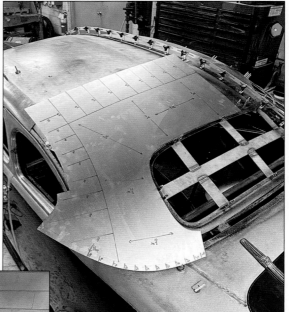

Seen from a higher angle, the panel and the way that it fits becomes obvious. Wagner uses Clecos and magnets to hold the panels in place.

The cut panel is laid out on the roof, complete with all of the measurements.

Wagner has now shaped the panel and is testing it for size and fitment.

Wagner's shaping of the panel is almost a perfect profile with what's left of the existing roof.

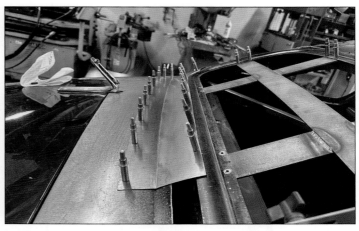

Wagner is shaping up a transition panel that goes between the decklid and the window frame.

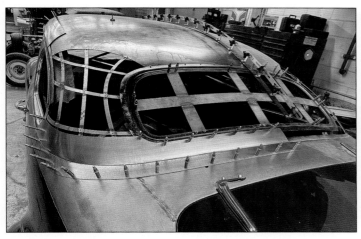

The filler panel is getting close to being done. It curves around the rear portion of the roof.

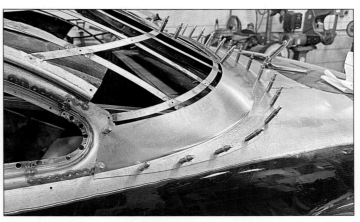

The decklid-to-window frame filler panel is Cleco'd into position. This photo also shows how the corner of the rear side window has been formed.

After giving it a coating of red Dykem, Wagner reinstalled the rear roof section and the rear window-to-decklid panel. Now, he is preparing to mark his cut lines.

This book was printed before Wagner finished the project. However, this photo shows the beauty of his work and his attention to detail.

PETE AND JAKE'S HOT ROD PARTS: BILLY F GIBBONS'S 1950 FORD SHOEBOX KOPPERHED

The association between the late Pete Chapouris and Billy F Gibbons of the band ZZ Top dates back to the early 1980s, when Pete and Jake's Hot Rod Parts built the chassis for Gibbons's Eliminator coupe. The two became fast friends and collaborated on several projects, including *Kopperhed*, which is Gibbons's hammered 1950 Ford Business Coupe.

According to Gibbons, the first car that he ever modified was his folks' 1949 Ford.

"I didn't have the money for a hot flat motor or one of the new overheads, so I did the cheap-out thing: I took it to the local muffler shop for a lowering job and a set of Glasspacks. Then, I [went to] Pep Boys for a bull nose and some phony whitewalls to make it look customized."

Years later, in 1994, when Gibbons and Chapouris were tight, Chapouris had Steve Stanford sketch up a chopped Shoebox. As far as I remember, it was a Chapouris concept that was understated with subtle modifications that looked as if it had come from the factory that way. The roof was chopped,

but it was only 3½ inches in the front and 3¼ inches in the back. The doors were extended 10 inches, and the rear side window was eliminated. However, the result looks like a contemporary factory concept—something that could have been destined for the auto show circuit but never destined for production.

A casual observer would barely notice the work. Yet, according to Chapouris, at the time, there had been 500 hours in the chop and another 1,000 hours in the finishing process. The majority of the chop was performed by Jim "Jake" Jacobs and

Rick "Speed" Lefever.

"I don't remember doing a whole lot," Lefever said. "I think it was more Jake than me, as he had more experience. I just followed his lead. I do remember that there was a lot—and I mean *a lot* (more than 20 feet)—of hammer welding across that roof."

Kopperhed was unveiled at a huge star-studded party at the Petersen Automotive Museum in 1995. In addition, the car was featured on the cover of *Hot Rod* magazine's January 1996 issue and *Rod & Custom* magazine's February 1996 issue. The car remains in Gibbons's collection.

This is what Billy F Gibbons's 1950 Ford Business Coupe stocker looked like when it arrived at Pete Chapouris's shop in Crestline, California. The work began at Chapouris's shop in Crestline, but when he moved to Pomona, California, he completed the project there.

By the time that this photo was taken, the doors were lengthened by 10 inches, the roof was sliced up, and the rear side windows were sectioned.

This shows exactly how the rear window was laid down and how the roof was sectioned and split. The upper rear side window frame was left intact, but it will change drastically.

The door was lengthened by 10 inches, and the B-pillar was fabricated to angle forward dramatically. The rear window will eventually be filled in with a panel.

The front posts were cut where the roof was split and on both sides of the peak. A split was also made across the roof about 8 inches back from the top of the windshield.

Partway through the project, Designer Steve Stanford (right) meets with Chapouris (left) and Jim "Jake" Jacobs to review progress. Stanford's rendering is all that the team had to reference.

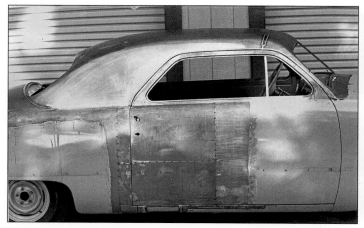

The rear side window was filled in with a sheet-metal panel. Note the work on the door and the panel behind the jamb.

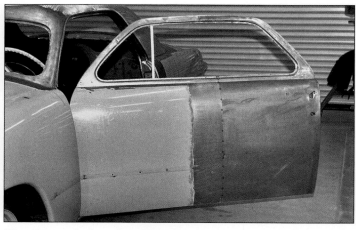

The door window frames take on an odd, conical profile when they're open. However, when they are closed and seated within the body, the fastback look that Stanford and the team wanted looks good.

Jacobs (left) and Rick Lefever hammer weld the various roof seams. This is time-consuming work, as you can only weld a little bit at a time, which prevents warpage. Note the blanket on the hood for protection.

The hammer-welded seams are shown in the roof. It looks like more than 20 feet of careful welding and hammering. Notice the clean-up grinding marks on the right side of the roof.

From this view above the back window, the roof was sliced. Laying down the rear window in this manner negated the need to cut curved glass.

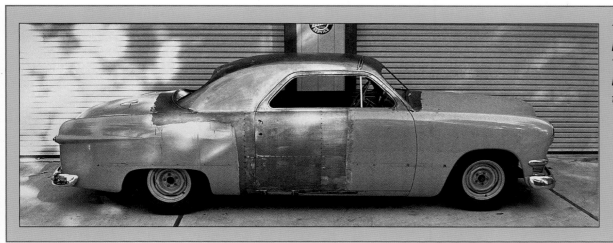

The car's profile looks stunning. The angled B-pillar looks natural when the door is closed.

When making the quarter windows, Jacobs showed high attention to detail. He made a fixture that could be used on both sides to ensure that the left and right sides were exactly the same.

The finished frames looked as factory as possible, which was exactly Jacobs's goal. The vent windows even retained their stainless deflectors.

Wearing a coat of black primer, Gibbons's Kopperhed is starting to look tough. The top of the windshield aligns with the side windows.

I was surprised that the outside decklid hinges were retained because they look a little odd sitting in that expanse of sheet metal, but that was Chapouris's style.

After the top chopping was completed, the late Mike Cardenas used a reciprocating saw to remove the stock front clip that apparently weighed less than its replacement.

In place of the stock front clip, Cardenas installed a fabricated assembly from Fat Man Fabrications that utilized Mustang II suspension components and ECI disc brakes.

The powertrain featured a rebuilt and slightly modified 1957 312-ci Y-block engine with three Ford carburetors, a Ford 3-speed/overdrive combination, and a narrowed Currie 9-inch rear end.

Tim Beard, a SO-CAL Speed Shop painter, begins the process of flatting and polishing the deep black paint on Kopperhed *beginning with 400-grit sandpaper and work-ing his way up to 3,000-grit sandpaper.*

The interior was masked off to prevent water from getting into locations where it's difficult to clean. Many shops forget this step.

As part of the final assembly, Peter Chapouris (Pete Chapouris's son) works on the interior while Cardenas works on the final wiring.

In September 1995, Kopperhed *was unveiled at a star-studded party at the Petersen Automotive Museum in Los Angeles as part of "The Rods & Custom of Billy F Gibbons" exhibit.*

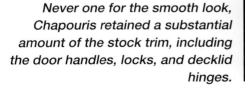

Never one for the smooth look, Chapouris retained a substantial amount of the stock trim, including the door handles, locks, and decklid hinges.

FABIAN VALDEZ: 1950 CHEVY STYLELINE

Fabian Valdez of Vintage Hammer Garage in San Bernardino, California, owns a beautifully chopped 1950 Chevy Styleline. Valdez cut his metal-shaping teeth on this car in the early 1990s, when he first started out in the business.

Unfortunately, I submitted many of the images of this car to a now-defunct print magazine, so most of those photographs are gone. However, enough photos survived to provide an overview of this superb chop, which was done to a car that is tricky to chop. Valdez's tutelage took place under the watchful eye of the late Bob Marianich. Marianich's career began in Detroit. First, he worked in the custom car business with the likes of the Alexander Brothers before graduating to his own business, which was called the Carriage Shop. He eventually worked for car manufacturers and played a role in the establishment of Toyota's Calty Design Research center in Newport Beach, California.

When I met Marianich and we photographed Valdez's Chevy, Marianich had a small studio and work space in Huntington Beach, California. It was cramped and tight for such a big project, but Marianich and Valdez pulled it off.

In 1950, Chevrolet still had a split windshield with flat glass, but Valdez opted for the one-piece windshield from a 1950 Oldsmobile. In addition, he shaved the gutters, shaved the hood and door handles, Frenched the headlights, rounded the door corners, and installed a modified 1948 Cadillac grille and side trim. In the back, the fenders were extended, tapered, and fitted with 1949 Buick Super Dynaflow taillights that were flipped into a vertical orientation. Note that the exhaust was rerouted to exit through the rear bumper.

As a result of his training in the OEM concept-car business, Marianich was methodical in his approach to metal shaping. He was a "measure thrice and cut once" kind of guy. In addition, he was meticulous in his cuts and rarely cut anything until he knew that he was making the right cut. It was great training for Valdez, who went on to open his own shop that specialized in metal shaping.

At this point, Marianich decided to move and left Valdez to finish the project. Tasks that remained included welding in the panel above the

Fabian Valdez of Vintage Hammer Garage in San Bernardino, California, stands next to his El Mirage–dusted 1950 Chevy that he and Bob Marianich chopped in the 1990s. It was Valdez's first chop.

The nicely shaped silhouette of the roof flows into the decklid. The well-shaped side windows flow with the door and the roof line. The the rear fenders were molded in, extended, tapered, and fitted with vertically mounted 1949 Buick Super Dynaflow taillights.

decklid, finishing the side panels, finishing the doors, the Frenching, the rear fenders, etc.

"It took me about a year to finish it," said Valdez. "My first trip in the car was to Paso in 1996, I think, and I won the Best Unfinished Custom award. A lot of the old timers came up and shook my hand, and I was elated by the response. Busy with my business, I parked [the car] for about 10 years. However, early in the 2000s I painted it my own mix of Newcastle Brown."

This land speed racer is not afraid to drive his creations even in the dust of El Mirage.

Sadly, most of the photos of Marianich working in his small Huntington Beach shop during the early days of Valdez's 1950 Chevy chop have been lost.

The driver-side rear window shows how well it was formed using cut pieces that were salvaged from the chop.

The door post was sectioned and aligned with the roof where the gutter was removed.

Marianich removed the rear window in one piece and laid it down to align with the new roof profile. He was meticulous in his attention to detail.

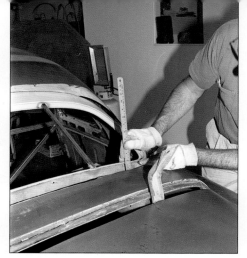

Marianich clamps the laid-down window frame into position. Notice how he welded in some 1/2-inch box section tubing to hold the frame in shape.

Meticulous with his measurements as well, Marianich rarely welded anything until he had measured and marked it and clamped or Cleco'd it into position.

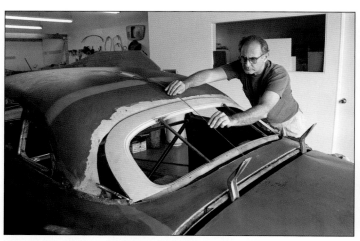

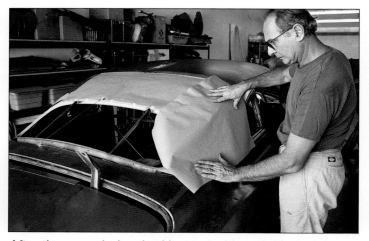

Welding rod works well to indicate how the lines are flowing. The trim bead where the roof joins the body will be eliminated eventually.

After the rear window had been positioned, Marianich used brown paper to make templates for the sheet metal. Although it is flat and only two-dimensional, the brown paper is a cheap and easy material to use to form templates.

Taped into position, this template for the rear quarter of the roof gave Marianich a good indication of the eventual shape of the panel.

The brown paper was transformed into sheet metal. The new panel was aligned with the roof and tacked to the rear window frame.

HOW TO CHOP TOPS

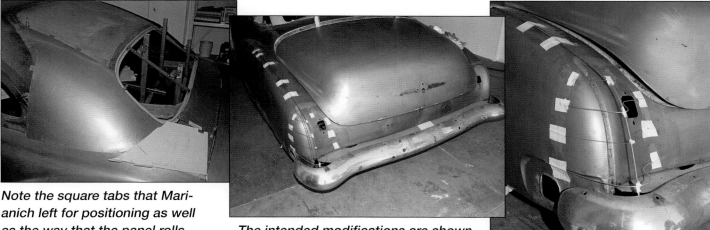

Note the square tabs that Marianich left for positioning as well as the way that the panel rolls down to the body, removing the trim bead line that is visible under the side window.

The intended modifications are shown to the rear fender and to the right of the stock fender. All mounting holes were eventually filled.

Welding rod was used to form the shape of the extension for the rear fender.

At this stage, Marianich moved his shop, leaving the young Valdez to finish his own project, which he did.

Valdez drove the Chevy unfinished for quite some time. He even won the Best Unfinished Custom award at the Paso Robles Car Show in 1996.

This classic custom car features cowl-mounted spotlights, a modified 1948 Cadillac grille, and frenched headlights that frame a shaved hood.

Classic Cadillac sombrero hubcaps were made between 1947 and 1952, and the 1948 Cadillac side trim compliments the modified 1948 Cadillac grille. Note that the wind wings still work.

MAX GRUNDY: 1960 DODGE DART PHOENIX AND 1961 CHRYSLER NEWPORT

It takes a bold man to cut into a 1950s or 1960s car, and artist Max Grundy is just such a man. Grundy hit the car scene in 2005 with his apocalyptic style of art, combining atomic culture, hot rods, and science fiction. It was bold and different with his catchy tag line "fear is the new beauty."

Grundy studied art and design and has a Bachelor of Fine Arts degree from Weber State University and a Master of Global Affairs degree with a minor in art history from Brigham Young University. In addition to being a teacher for 10 years and a freelancer for more than 25 years, he was

the official feature artist of the SEMA Show from 2013 to 2015. He customizes cars that have a high level of difficulty, which has included cutting up Chrysler Designer Virgil Exner's "Forward Look" cars. He has succeeded in making them even more outrageous than when they were new.

1960 Dodge Dart Phoenix

The 1960 Dodge Dart Phoenix was Chrysler's effort to position the brand above Plymouth and below Chrysler. Since Grundy had experience chopping the top on this type of car, it was less of a challenge the second time around.

When it came to the 1960 Dodge Dart Phoenix, Grundy was well experienced, having already chopped a 1961 Chrysler Newport with the aid of his Australian friend Justin Hills. However, a significant amount of additional work was involved with the Dart, as Grundy

swapped out the rear fenders for those from a 1960 Chrysler as well. That move necessitated alterations to the front fenders.

It was a massive project that I began photographing before Grundy moved from California to Kansas, where the metalwork was finished.

The Dodge has a sail panel that Grundy wanted to keep. While doing so, he wanted to reduce the arch to a more streamline curve as the top came down. He also wanted to remove the dogleg.

This shows the dogleg in the sail panel that Grundy wanted to remove. In addition, the lines in the existing sail panel and the roof will be cut.

Grundy likes to make lightweight fiberglass molds of the front and rear glass. This allows him to get a rough idea of the front and rear glass and to see the car's profile.

The next step is to brace the rear window using square stock so that it is a solid piece that will be easy to remove when the top chop is done.

Note the amount of internal bracing that Grundy installed to tie the car together while he cut off the roof.

Grundy uses tape rather than marker because the tape sticks to the metal and keeps the measurement (instead of marker possibly being rubbed off).

Grundy shows how he wants the arch of the window trim to change as the top comes down. He's checking to see how much the stainless steel flexes.

The last 12 to 18 inches of gutter were cut from the body so that Grundy could lower the top and use the attached section as a guide to help him form the new contour.

Grundy marked some vertical lines and made a wood template for how he wants the new shape to look.

Grundy flattened out the rear section of rain gutter and welded it back into place, completing the flow and eliminating the dogleg.

This shows how the top will come down after the yellow sections are removed. With the slit cuts making a spine, the top goes forward onto the new shape.

These before (top) and after (bottom) photos show how the removal of the dogleg improves the flow of the C-pillar.

More Details from Max Grundy

"This area is my primary concern, as I want this spot to have a new flow," Max Grundy said. "Personally, I find this to be the case with most top chops. Whether it's a finned car or a 1950 Mercury, the area between the back windows and the middle of the roof is the area that needs the most reshaping—along with the quarter window.

"I try to be close to stock length, which usually requires this area to be angled up to land in the approximate stock location. That is why I made the multiple verticals marks. These will actually be cut into slits along the sail panel to create a spine. So, as the top comes down on the A-Pillars, pulling the back forward to flatten it out, the rear crown is reduced. On these 'Forward Look' top chops, you don't even have to remove material from the C-pillar. It simply lowers down into a new contour like a centipede effect."

Grundy removes the reinforced rear window. Generally, he cuts about an inch back from where the stainless would attach.

Removing the roof skin allowed Grundy to cut the inner structure for recontouring. It's helpful to keep the side supports in place so that each side moves equally.

Using a cut-off wheel or a saw, Grundy makes the vertical cuts for the spine. The material is about 5 inches to cut through.

After these cuts, Grundy will make a new sail panel. The cross-brace in the roof helps hold both sides together to move the same amount.

Grundy takes care to not cut through the last layer of steel because it holds the spine together. He wasn't able to avoid cutting through the rain gutter.

Grundy uses an angle grinder to cut through the multi-layered A-pillar. Note the tie strap that is being used for alignment.

More Details from Max Grundy

"The interesting thing about this approach is that your top never has to be 100-percent removed," Max Grundy said. "The C-pillars don't have to be cut free completely. Instead, we cut the front and let the rear flow down. When using this technique, you may have to cut the C-pillar, depending on the amount of material removed and if the flow is not to your desired look."

The new shape of the top is visible after the A-pillars have been cut. Note that the screen surround is tapered and the posts do note align.

More Details from Max Grundy

"At this stage, the rear portion of the top is pulled a little tight," Max Grundy said. "So, I'll cut the C-pillar free, allowing the rear post to come forward a few inches and the radius of the curve to be perfectly achieved."

To align the A-pillars, Grundy cut slots in the upper and bottom corners and pulled the top of the posts out to align with the bottoms.

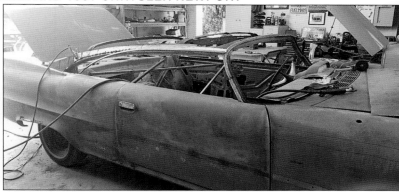

The top is beginning to take shape. However, the A-pillars no longer align, and relief cuts will need to be made in the frame.

The new, lower profile looks good. Note that the A-pillars remain out of alignment for the time being.

More Details from Max Grundy

"I made two relief cuts in the top and bottom of each A-pillar," Max Grundy said. "This allows you to align the posts perfectly. Ratchet straps work well if you need to put muscle into it. Once it has been tacked into place, take a cross-measurement of the windshield to make sure both sides are equal. If they are equal, you know they are perfect on each side. In addition, we have welded the roof skin back on to better see the profile. Note also where we cut off the roof skin at the car's natural sail panel area."

The roof has been separated from the windshield frame and is being held aloft by small blocks of wood.

This shows how the lowered roof matches with the plywood template that was created earlier. It also shows how the roof drops in behind the sail panel.

More Details from Max Grundy

"We like to make fiberglass molds of the front and rear glass," Max Grundy said. "These allow you to put in a rough idea of your front and rear glass quickly (and with a much lighter object) to see your car's profile. You can move [the fiberglass] in and out very easily with a mold instead of the heavy glass.

"The fiberglass form can be made easily with products from a paint supply store. Coat your windshield in spray grease of some kind. Then, lay the wet fiberglass/fiber onto the glass. I also reinforce with steel rod. It's a bit more work for these molds, but I find it useful because these windshields were used in almost all 1960 to 1961 Mopars."

Grundy made several relief cuts about 24 inches long to allow the roof to spread evenly and flatten. This streamlines the car top in the rear.

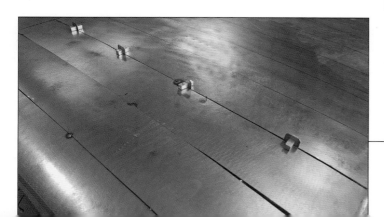

Grundy's photoshop rendering (bottom) is shown versus the real chop. Photoshop can be used to test an idea before cutting metal.

The top photo was taken before the 3-inch chop, and the bottom photo was taken after the chop. You can see that most of the reshaping happened in the roof between the B-pillars and C-pillars.

The relief splits in the rear half of the roof are shown.

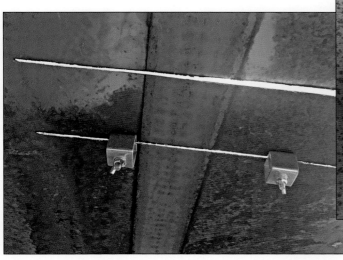

These are Chicago Electric butt-welding clamps that are used to securely hold material while you weld. They are available from several companies, including Harbor Freight.

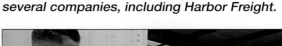

This is the split rear roof section that can be seen when looking up from the inside of the car.

The Dart has been rolled into the sun so that the car can be seen from a distance. Air was let out of the tires to simulate the car being lowered. Although this method is crude, it helped Grundy see the profile.

Grundy gestures to the finned back end of a 1960 Chrysler that he will graft on to the 1960 Dodge. The Chrysler is much longer than the Dodge.

This shows where the 1960 Dodge had to be cut to graft on the 1960 Chrysler fins. Both cars were the same width, and the swap went well.

It's a brave man who will do this to a 1960s car, but Grundy is a talented artist with a great vision.

Grundy's Dodge is shown with the rear clip removed. Note the dummy fiberglass rear windshield that was used in the mock-up process.

Grundy manually stripped the paint from the donor car and enjoyed seeing how well they fit together. However, the Chrysler was about 10 inches longer than the Dodge.

After the Chrysler fins were added to the Dodge, the car was moved back out in the sun for a review.

At this point in the project, there is still a large amount of work to do to make the front fenders work with the Chrysler doors and rear clip.

The sail panel is being spot welded into place. The sail panel is concave, which mimics the stock car.

A section is being cut out of the front fenders where Grundy had to add the edge that continues onward from the 1960 Chrysler's doors.

Grundy welded the new sail panel, and the overall flow of the top is pleasing as it drops down into the decklid.

The section that was removed from the front fender is shown. The removal was necessary to continue the fender line from the Chrysler doors.

Grundy uses duct tape to hold the section of the fender in position.

The section of the fender to extend the fender line has been installed. However, it still needs to flow into the headlight nacelles.

The car has been moved back into the sunshine to review the modified front fenders. There's still work to do, but it has great confluence between the roof and the fender.

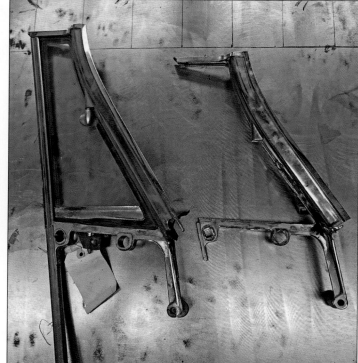

Bernardo Blanco of Bernie's Auto Glass installs the windshield. Grundy likes to install the windshield when the car is in bare metal. In case there are any fitment problems, it's easier to shape metal than glass.

To chop the wind wings, Grundy trimmed off the desired amount from the bottom, moved the hardware upward, and rewelded the parts.

1961 Chrysler Newport

At the time of compiling content for this book, Max had not painted the 1960 Dodge, so I included his previous chop of a 1961 Chrysler Newport, which was finished a few years ago. This shows what a finished version of one of these "Exner extreme" cars looks like with a lowered lid.

Introduced in 1961, the Newport was a large and comfortable two- or four-door vehicle that was modestly priced (when compared to Chrysler's 300, New Yorker, and Imperial). It was the last year of the big-fin cars that were designed by Virgil Exner.

Grundy's first trip into "Exner space" was when he debuted the 1961 *Khrysler Kustom* at the 2019 SEMA Show. While the original concept was designed by Grundy, the 3-D rendering was created by the Moffitt Brothers (actually husband Anthony and wife Jesse) of northwest Arkansas.

The 3-inch chop was executed by Grundy and his friend Justin Hills of Hills & Co., which is based in New South Wales, Australia. These two also handled the bodywork along with Shawn Campbell, Donnie Potter, and Pete Moore. The glass was cut by "Big" Al Backes of Pomona, California.

This 1961 Chrysler Windsor two-door hardtop looked pretty nice in Grundy's shop before he cut it down.

Grundy's jumping-off point was to make a cardboard template of the side windows to show what the car would look like with the top chopped.

Grundy took a quick reinforced fiberglass mold of the front and rear glass that is lighter and easier to use than glass when doing the chop.

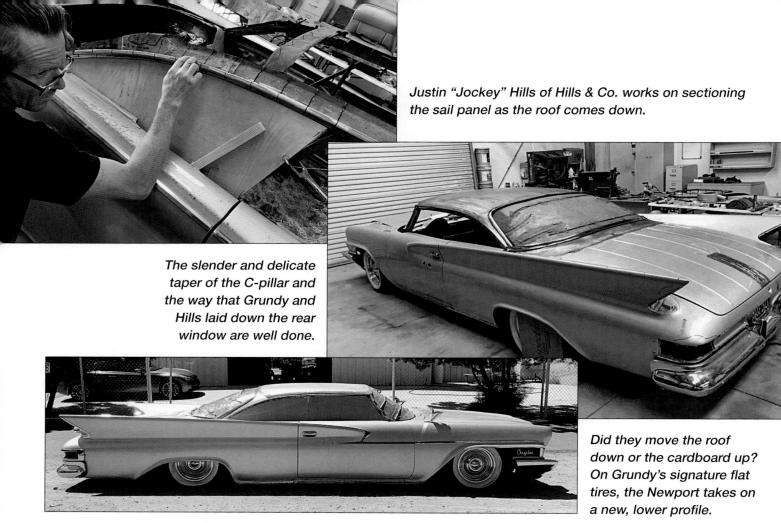

Justin "Jockey" Hills of Hills & Co. works on sectioning the sail panel as the roof comes down.

The slender and delicate taper of the C-pillar and the way that Grundy and Hills laid down the rear window are well done.

Did they move the roof down or the cardboard up? On Grundy's signature flat tires, the Newport takes on a new, lower profile.

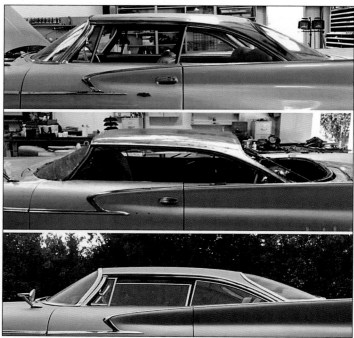

Photoshop is a great tool to see what things were (top), what they look like in process of a top chop (middle), and how they will be (bottom).

Finished, painted, and photographed by Mike Harrington, Grundy's chopped 1961 Chrysler Newport is as cool as it gets. (Photo Courtesy Mike Harrington)

CHAPTER 15

GLASS CUTTING

Anyone can chop a top, and some people can also weld it back together, but it takes a real craftsman to cut the glass.

The first thing to know is that you can cut laminated glass, but you can't cut tempered glass. Laminated glass was introduced in the 1920s, and it is basically two sheets of glass with a sheet of polyvinyl butyral (PVB) sandwiched between them. Tempered glass, on the other hand, is single ply and is treated by rapid heating and cooling to make it tough.

When tempered glass breaks, it shatters into thousands of pieces. When laminated glass breaks, it doesn't shatter because it is held together by the PVB. Laminated glass is typically used for windshields, and tempered glass is used for side and rear windows.

Starting in 1927, Henry Ford was the first manufacturer to begin using Triplex glass in his cars. In May 1931, laminated safety glass became optional in all windows.

If you're chopping an early car with flat glass, you will have fewer problems than if you were cutting curved glass for a 1950s or 1960s car. In addition, if you happen to break flat glass, it's a nuisance, but it's not the disaster that breaking a curved, possibly tinted windshield can be.

Windshields on the internet can cost as low as $150 for a tinted '55 Chevy Bel Air windshield. To get an idea of prices and to find a wide range of glass and accessories, visit the Bob's Classic Auto Glass website (bobsclassicautoglass.com). For example, a tinted windshield for a 1964–1966 Chevy/GMC truck can be purchased for about $365. Bob's Classic Auto Glass ships all over the world, which can be helpful for anyone who is chopping a top a long distance from a city with a competent glass cutter. The company will cut custom flat glass, but it no longer cuts curved glass. Bob's Classic Auto Glass is located in Blachly, Oregon.

Another company worth checking is vintageglass.com. I found its website difficult to navigate, but the product is made in the USA, and it has locations across the country. Another company is autocityglass.com.

While performing research for this chapter, I viewed many videos on the internet, and those by Chris Blattie of Montana Glass and Shower Door stood out. Blattie got his start 20 years ago when he cut the back glass for his 1952 Styleline Deluxe out of a 1994 Toyota Camry windshield. He kindly allowed us to document his process. In addition, you can send Blattie a template, and he will cut and ship the glass to you.

Typically, traditional glass cutters cut the glass using a professional, self-oiling cutter with a diamond wheel to cut the two outer pieces of glass. Then, they heat the plastic filler and slice it with a tool that is thin and sharp. They typically begin by removing the corners to eliminate stress points, run the cutter, open up the cut, flip over the glass, and make the exact same cut on the other side. Then, using denatured alcohol, they heat the plastic, which is then cut with a blade.

Finishing the edge is usually done with a sander, but I have seen it done with an angle grinder (polishing from 220 to 400 grit.) There are even special diamond wheels from companies such as Rodex that make the job easier for the DIYer.

After the glass has been cut, test fit it in the frame and see if there are areas that need trimming. Of course, if you have had your glass cut and shipped, the trimming will be up to you. So, be careful and always use safety eyewear. Meanwhile, remember these three things: 1) A 3-inch roof chop doesn't necessarily mean a 3-inch chop to the glass, 2) Watch all of the instructional videos, especially Chris Blattie at Montana Glass, and 3) Understand that most glass cutters do not guarantee their work. (If the windshield breaks or cracks it's your problem—not theirs.)

Chris Blattie of Montana Glass was sent a pattern by his customer for a chopped 1961 Chevy Suburban. However, the customer wanted it cut at the bottom, and Blattie typically cuts off the top.

Blattie indicates the tight curved part of the windshield. It gets tricky at this location because there is a lot of stress in the glass because it's so curved.

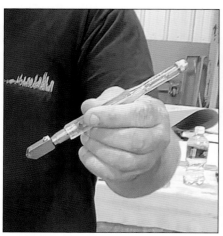

The correct professional glass cutter is essential. Blattie uses an oil-filled, diamond-wheel cutter from C. R. Laurence, which costs about $75.

Blattie cuts from the center outward. He said that you must use even pressure and not skip or break your cut because the score is the most important part of the job.

Blattie has a pair of special, forged steel Drop Jaw glass-breaking pliers from C. R. Laurence with this raised area that he uses to tap the glass.

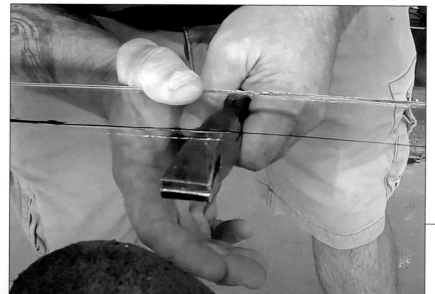

At this point, the glass has only been scored on one side. Next, Blattie takes his Drop Jaw pliers and taps upward, (behind the score). His thumb on the edge keeps it from bouncing.

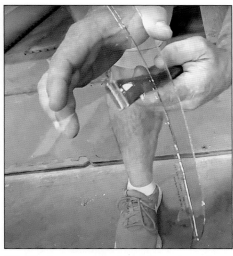

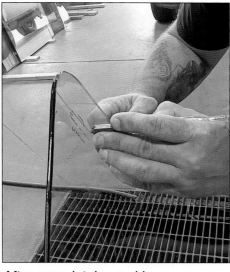

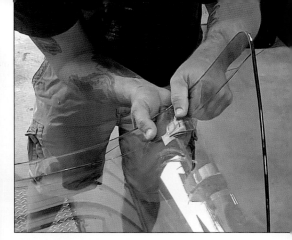

Blattie began cracking the glass from the center but moved to the end until the crack went off of the line, so he went back to the center and cracked outward to the end.

After completely cracking one side, Blattie flipped over the glass and scored the other side, scoring exactly on top of the first score.

Again, Blattie uses his pliers to crack the glass. He said that it's usually easier on the second side and that you can probably do it with your hands if you make sure that both sides have been broken all the way through.

Next, Blattie soaks the cut line with denatured alcohol and sets fire to it to soften the plastic between the glass.

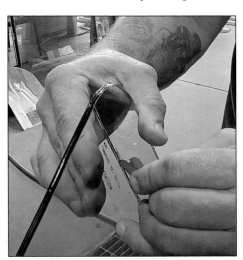

Blattie uses a razor blade to cut through the plastic. The area where there is lettering can be tricky, he said. The better you scored the glass, the easier this is.

After the plastic has been cut all of the way through, the glass will fall away. Then, grind down and smooth the edges.

Scan this QR code with your smartphone to learn about chop school.

Source Guide

Auto City Classic Inc.
28433 Highway 65 NE
Isanti, MN 55040
800-828-2212
Email: autocity@att.net
AutoCityClassic.com

Bernie's Custom Glass
910 N. San Fernando Rd.
Los Angeles, CA 90065
323-401-1961

Bob's Classic Auto Glass
21170 OR-36
Blachly, OR 97412
800-624-2130
Email:
  info@bobsclassicautoglass.com
BobsClassicAutoGlass.com

Brookville Roadster
718 Albert Rd.
Brookville, OH 45309
937-833-4422
BrookvilleRoadster.com

Cornfield Customs Ltd.
5907 Deerfield Rd.
Milford, OH 45150
513-575-4322
cornfieldcustomsltd.com

CR Laurence Co. Inc.
2503 E. Vernon Ave.
Los Angeles, CA 90058
800-421-6144
CRlaurance.com

CW Moss
420 W Chapman Ave.
Orange, CA 92866
1-800-322-1932
Cwmoss.com

Davis Haus of Style (Joel Davis)
Email: Pinstriper40@hotmail.com
Facebook.com/davis-haus-of-style
ChopClass.com

Max Grundy
818-445-1730
MaxGrundy.com

Justin Hills & Co.
2/50 Hargreaves Dr.
Taree, NSW 2430, Australia
+61 2 6551 6777
Email: Justin@JustinHills.com.au
JustinHills.com.au

Hollywood Hot Rods
2617 N. San Fernando Blvd.
Burbank, CA 91504
818-842-6900
HollywoodHotRods.com

Kennedy Brothers Bomb Factory
1000 E. End
Pomona, CA 91766

Lazze Inc.
939 Highland Way
  Suite A-B
Grover Beach, CA 93433
805-668-2045
925-899-0866
Lazzemetalshaping.com

Leading Edge Machine & Design
4395 Highland Meadows Pkwy.
Windsor, CO 80550
402-660-8289
Leadingedgemad.com

Larry Erickson Design
Email: Lerickson32@gmail.com

Mick's Paint
1357 East Grand Ave.
Pomona, CA 91766
310-947-6727
MicksPaint.com

Rick Lefever
1367 East Grand Ave.
Pomona, CA 91766
626-825-2079

Montana Glass & Shower Door
504 Bernard St.
Billings, Montana
406-690-6467
Email: cblattie@aol.com
montanaglassandshowerdoor.com

Rolling Bones Hot Rod Shop
47 S. Greenfield Rd.
Greenfield Center, NY 12833
518-893-2646
RollingBonesHotRodShop.com

The Tin Man's Garage Inc.
500 E. State St.
Sycamore, IL 60178
815-991-5308
Thetinmansgarage.com

United Pacific
3788 E. Conant St.
Long Beach, CA 90808
800-790-6988
UPAuto.com

Veazie Bros. Fabrication
1359 E. Grand Ave.
Pomona, CA 91766

VintageGlass
Headquarters in Florida
(locations in Ohio, Kentucky,
New York, and Oklahoma and
warehouses with glass inventory
in another 45 states)
888-446-2191
Email: Mail@VintageGlass.com
VintageGlass.com

Walden Speed Shop
1040 Price St.
Pomona, CA 91766
909-623-3747
WaldenSpeedShop.com